QUICK
Vegetarian Dishes

QUICK
Vegetarian Dishes

Kurma Dasa

CHAKRA PRESS

Chakra Press

10 Rochester St., Botany, NSW 2019, Australia
email: austbbt@attglobal.net

Chakra Press is an imprint of the Bhaktivedanta Book Trust, Australia

Publisher	Naresvara Dasa
Photography	Peter Bailey, (Melbourne)
Food Styling	Jane Borthwick
Art Direction and Design	Ross Goode (Rama Prasad Dasa)
Editor	Carol D'Costa (Krishna rupa dasi)
Food Preparation	Kurma Dasa, Ananda Yukta devi dasi, Naresvara Dasa

ISBN 0 9578345 00

DEDICATION

This book is dedicated to my spiritual master,
His Divine Grace A. C. Bhaktivedanta Swami Prabhupada,
who taught us how to enter into a loving transaction with
Krishna by preparing and offering vegetarian foods with devotion
and accepting the remnants as *prasadam*.

Acknowledgments

Once again I would like to thank my publisher, Naresvara Dasa, for making this book a reality. This is the fourth book we have worked on together, and hopefully not the last.

My old friend Ram Prasad Dasa is responsible for the book's beautiful and innovative design and layout. His dedication to the project and hard labour certainly paid off.

It was a great pleasure to again work with Peter Bailey who took the wonderful photographs and was, as usual, solid as a rock at all times. The inspirational styling is the very professional work of Jane Borthwick.

A special thanks goes to my wife, Ananda Yukta, for her assistance and encouragement at all stages of the book's development.

Aniruddha Dasa was kind enough to allow the crew comfortable accommodation throughout the final weeks. Thanks to Krishna rupa dasi (Carol D'Costa), the editor, Drutakarma Dasa for the *Introduction*, and Trevor Absalom for the *Index*. Ranjit Dasa from Bhaktivedanta Archives provided the photograph of Srila Prabhupada on the dedication page.

Britta Meyer, Yuka Watanabe, and Sienna Clark assisted in the studio.

A final thanks goes to Casa Alfresco of Chadstone, Roost of Malvern, Market Import of Armadale, The Big Duck & Fish Co. of Fitzroy, Table Talk of Camberwell, Home & Abroad of South Yarra and Signorino of Richmond.

Table of Contents

Introduction

Kurma Dasa, Australia's vegetarian *guru*, has done it again. His first two highly successful books, *Great Vegetarian Dishes* and *Cooking with Kurma*, along with their entertaining television series, made him a culinary celebrity worldwide. His latest, *Quick Vegetarian Dishes*, is sure to add to his reputation as the high priest of vegetarian cooking.

Kurma's message in *Quick Vegetarian Dishes* is refreshingly simple: life in the fast lane doesn't necessarily mean life in the fast food line. Even if your life is moving at Web speed, you can, with Kurma's expert guidance, quickly prepare something hot and fresh, stunningly original and tasty, for yourself, for two, or a few others, almost as quickly as you can order out. In *Quick Vegetarian Dishes*, you'll find the gastronomical equivalent of sound bites—taste bites, essential gourmet vegetarian delights that deliver the most palatable results with the least amount of time and effort. If you're the type of person that jumps on a plane with only carry-on luggage, this is the cookbook for you. You'll be in and out of the kitchen in record time.

Like life today, the fare in *Quick Vegetarian Dishes* is fast, stylish, variegated, and multicultural. Kurma has chosen a tantalising array of international dishes to showcase your speed-cooking talents. Just reading over the recipe list for each chapter is enough to make you cancel the restaurant reservations and pick up a saucepan.

When I called Kurma a vegetarian *guru* and high priest, I was not just using some interesting figures of speech. Kurma's vegetarian cooking is deeply rooted in his spiritual practice. Back in 1971, Kurma became the disciple of one of India's most respected *gurus*, His Divine Grace Srila A. C. Bhaktivedanta Swami Prabhupada. In addition to being an accomplished scholar of Vedic literature and the world's leading teacher of *bhakti-yoga*, the *yoga* of devotion, Srila Prabhupada was also an expert cook who delighted his disciples with his *samosas, pakoras* and other exotic Indian preparations.

From his *guru*, Kurma learned that cooking is an act of love and devotion. In India's timeless spiritual classic, the *Bhagavad-gita*, Krishna, the Supreme Personality of Godhead, says that He accepts vegetarian foods prepared and offered to Him with love and devotion. Such food becomes infused with spiritual energy, and free from all the effects of *karma*. Indeed, those who practise *bhakti-yoga* will eat only food that has first been offered to Krishna.

Such food, technically called *prasadam* (mercy), gives not only nourishment but enlightenment. Shri Chaitanya Mahaprabhu, the most recent incarnation of Krishna, once said that the ingredients of such food are material but when they are tasted by Krishna, they become full of all spiritual qualities.

If you wish to follow Kurma in adding a spiritual dimension to your vegetarian cooking, it's easy to do. Prepare one or more of the recipes

Above: His Divine Grace A.C. Bhaktivedanta Swami Prabhupada. *Founder-Acharya of The International Society for Krishna Consciousness.*

Rama Rama, Hare Hare. (For instructions on how to perform a more elaborate offering with additional Sanskrit *mantras*, contact the publisher.)

If you do, you'll be on your way to making the cooking and eating of Kurma specialities (such as his *Oven-fried Potato Wedges with Quick Tomato Chutney*) into a totally spiritual experience.

in the book, but don't taste anything while you are cooking. The idea is that Krishna should taste it first. On these pages, you'll find pictures of Shrila Prabhupada, Shri Caitanya, and Shri Krishna, which can be used for making offerings.

For the purpose of making an offering, it is best to reserve a special plate and cup that are not used for eating. Place a little of each preparation on the plate and put the beverage (or some water) in the cup. Place the plate and cup before the pictures (you can stand this book up in front of the plate, opened to the pictures). Then simply ask Shrila Prabhupada, Lord Chaitanya, and Lord Krishna to accept the offering. After that, you can chant the Hare Krsna *mantra* three times: Hare Krishna, Hare Krishna, Krishna Krishna, Hare Hare, Hare Rama, Hare Rama,

Michael A. Cremo
(Drutakarma Dasa)

Co-author of *The Higher Taste: A Guide to Gourmet Vegetarian Cooking and a Karma-Free Diet, Divine Nature: A Spiritual Perspective on the Environmental Crisis,* and *Forbidden Archeology: The Hidden History of the Human Race.*

16 August, 2000
Los Angeles, California

Above Left: Lord Chaitanya along with His associates
Above: Radha and Krishna

How to Measure and Use the Recipes

Measurement of Volume

To conveniently use these recipes, you will require a set of graduated spoons (¼ teaspoon, ½ teaspoon, 1 teaspoon and 1 tablespoon) and a set of graduated cups (¼ cup, ⅓ cup, ½ cup and 1 cup). A glass or plastic liquid measuring container, usually containing cup, pint and litre markings will also be handy. Note that there is some difference between Australian, American and British cup and spoon measurements, as explained below.

Teaspoons: Australian, American and British teaspoons all hold approximately 5ml.

Tablespoons: Tablespoon measurements given in this book are standard Australian tablespoons, holding 20ml. The American standard tablespoon holds 14.2ml and the British standard tablespoon holds 17.7ml. American readers are advised to heap their tablespoons and British readers to slightly heap their tablespoons.

Cups: Cup measurements given in this book are standard Australian cups, which hold 250ml. The American and British cups hold 240ml. Therefore American and British readers should generously fill their standard measuring cups, and in the case of liquids, should add 2 teaspoons extra for every cup required.

Measurement of Weight

All measurements of weight in this book have been given in metric with imperial in brackets. Thus: **140g (5 ounces) butter**

Measurement of Temperature

Accurate temperatures are indicated for baking and for some deep-frying. In this book, measurements are given first in Celsius, then in Fahrenheit. Thus: **185°C/365°F**
A cooking thermometer is a useful accessory.

Baking: All recipes were tested in a fan-forced electric oven. If you are baking in a conventional oven, add on approximately 5 minutes to the baking times. However, this should only serve as a guide because oven performance varies considerably.

Measurement of Length

Measurements are given in centimetres with inches in parentheses. Thus:
1.25cm (½-inch)
25cm (10 inches)

In Conclusion

Note the following suggestions to get the best out of these recipes:
• Read the entire recipe first and obtain all the ingredients before commencing to cook. Measure all the ingredients beforehand and place them where they can be easily reached.
• All measurements for the spoons and cups are level unless otherwise specified.
• For information about unfamiliar ingredients or techniques, see *Glossary*.

Special Notes for American Cooks

The following list will clarify any confusion that may arise because of the different cooking terms and ingredient names used in Australia and America.

baking tray	baking sheet
beetroot	beet
bicarbonate of soda	baking soda
biscuit	cookie
cake tin	cake/baking pan
capsicums	peppers
caster sugar	fine granulated sugar
chickpeas	garbanzo beans
continental parley	flat-leaf parsley
cornflour	cornstarch
frying pan	skillet
grill	broil
icing sugar	confectioner's sugar
plain flour	all-purpose flour
raw sugar	turbinado sugar
self-raising flour	self-rising flour
semolina	farina
sultanas	golden raisins
wholemeal flour	wholewheat flour

Entrees
and Appetisers

Inari-zushi is a popular Japanese takeaway finger food. Slices of deep-fried tofu are opened and used as pouches for sushi rice. They have an intriguing flavour that is at once savoury and sweet. To make them, you will need thin, deep-fried tofu slices called abura-age-dofu found in a well-stocked Asian supermarket.

Sushi Rice in Tofu Pouches (Inari-zushi)

makes 16

8 rectangular pieces, 5cm x 10cm
(2 inches x 4 inches), or 16
square pieces 5cm x 5cm
(2 inches x 2 inches) thin, deep-fried tofu slices (*abura-age dofu*)

3 cups cooked, cooled and seasoned *sushi* rice (see recipe in this chapter)

6 teaspoons sesame seeds, dry-roasted in a frying pan until golden

pickled ginger slices *(gari)*

soy sauce for dipping

Prepare the tofu slices: if the *abura-age-dofu* comes sealed with flavoured juices, drain and use straight from the packet. Otherwise if they are dry-packed, rinse them in boiling water and pat them dry to remove excess oil.

Cut the tofu slices: if the *abura-age-dofu* is rectangular, cut each piece into two squares. If the tofu comes already cut into squares, it requires no cutting.

Fold the *sushi* rice with the toasted sesame seeds. Moisten your hands.

Form the *sushi* rice into 16 golf ball-sized lumps.

Open each tofu pouch by carefully pulling the cut edge apart. Fill each tofu pouch with a ball of rice. Do not fill the pouch too tightly or else it will break. Wrap the edges of the pouch around the rice to form an enclosed pouch. Place onto a serving tray with the folded edge down.

Serve at room temperature accompanied with pickled ginger and soy sauce for dipping.

Note: Instead of roasted sesame seeds, try the following alternative flavourings—finely-chopped carrot and lotus root, Japanese pepper *(sansho)*, poppy seeds with finely chopped cucumber, or lemon zest.

Corn tortillas, dried chipotle chilies and smoked hot paprika are available in well-stocked supermarkets, Latin American stores or gourmet grocers.

Tortilla Triangles
with Smoky Avocado Salsa

serves 4

4 corn tortillas
oil for frying

Salsa

2 firm ripe avocados, about 250g
   (9 ounces) each, halved, peeled
   and chopped
3 tablespoons finely shredded
   inner leaves of iceberg lettuce
1 small green chili, seeded and
   sliced into fine julienne
¼ teaspoon yellow asafetida
   powder
2 tablespoons lime juice
2 tablespoons finely-chopped
   coriander leaves
1 medium-sized dried *chipotle* chili,
   finely chopped and reconstituted
   in a few tablespoons hot water
   for 15 minutes, or 1 teaspoon
   smoky hot Spanish paprika
¼ teaspoon ground white pepper
½ teaspoon salt

Cut each tortilla into six wedges. Heat some oil in a small frying pan. **Shallow-fry** the wedges until golden and crisp. Drain on paper towels.

Combine all the *salsa* ingredients in a bowl and mix gently.
Serve with the tortilla wedges as an appetizer.

Succulent homemade panir cheese is a breeze to make. Here it combines beautifully with crisp green beans, juicy orange sweet potatoes and baby spinach leaves with tangy sesame dressing.

Panir Fillets with
Sweet Potato & Baby Beans

serves 4–6

600g (1 pound 3 ounces) orange-fleshed sweet potatoes, peeled and cut into 2.5cm (1-inch) cubes

200g (2½ ounces) baby green beans, trimmed

1 tablespoon olive oil

½ teaspoon yellow asafetida powder

600g (1 pound 3 ounces) homemade curd cheese *(panir)*, made from 5 litres/quarts milk, sliced (recipe follows)

100g (3½ ounces) baby spinach leaves

Dressing

1½ tablespoons lemon juice

2 tablespoons extra-virgin olive oil

2 teaspoons seeded or dijon mustard

1 teaspoon sugar

1 tablespoon pan-toasted sesame seeds

1 teaspoon salt

freshly-ground black pepper

Whisk together the dressing ingredients, and set aside.

Steam the sweet potatoes and beans separately until tender. Drain and keep warm.

Heat the olive oil in a frying pan over moderate heat. When quite warm, sprinkle in the yellow asafetida powder and fry briefly.

Fry the slices of *panir* for 1 or 2 minutes on each side, or until they are a pale golden colour. Carefully remove and set aside on paper towels.

Combine the pan-fried *panir*, the sweet potatoes, beans, spinach and dressing, and toss gently.

Serve warm, or at room temperature, with a grinding of fresh black pepper.

Homemade Curd Cheese (Panir)

5 litres/quarts fresh milk

3–4 cups yogurt or 6–8 tablespoons lemon juice

Heat the milk to boiling point in a heavy-based saucepan.

Gradually stir in three-quarters of the yogurt or lemon juice. The milk should separate into chunky curds, leaving a greenish liquid residue called whey. If not completely separated, add a little more yogurt or lemon juice. Drape a double thickness of cheesecloth over a colander sitting in the sink.

Scoop out the curds with a slotted spoon and place them in the cheesecloth. Pour the whey and whatever curds that remain in the saucepan into the cheesecloth. Gather the ends of the cloth together and hold the bag of curd cheese under cold running water for 30 seconds. Twist the bag tightly to squeeze out extra whey, and return it to the colander.

Press under a heavy weight for 10–15 minutes. Carefully remove the curd cheese from the cloth. Your *panir* is ready.

Butter-soft avocados, crisp snow peas and sweet mangos combine
beautifully in this very unusual entrée, which also doubles as a light lunch.

Pan-fried Tofu with Mango & Snow Peas

serves 6

1 large ripe, firm mango, halved,
seeded and cut into long strips

1 large ripe avocado, halved,
seeded and cut into long strips

1 tablespoon lime juice

100g (3½ ounces) snow peas,
trimmed

1 tablespoon olive oil

1 teaspoon yellow asafetida
powder

300g (11 ounces) large cakes of
fried tofu, sliced into
thin squares

1 medium-sized red chili, seeded
and sliced julienne

40g (1½ ounces) snow pea
sprouts

Dressing

1 tablespoon soy sauce

3 tablespoons olive oil

3 teaspoons balsamic vinegar

½ teaspoon *sambal oelek*

¼ cup lemon or lime juice

1 tablespoon palm sugar, grated

Whisk together all the dressing ingredients in a small bowl.

Combine the mango and avocado strips with 1 tablespoon of lime juice in a large bowl.

Blanch the snow peas in boiling water for 1 or 2 minutes, or until bright green and crisp-tender. Drain and set aside.

Heat 1 tablespoon of oil in a frying pan over moderate heat, sprinkle in the yellow asafetida powder, sauté momentarily. Briefly fry the slices of tofu in the fragrant oil. Remove the pan from the heat.

Fold in half the fried tofu with the mango and avocado, along with the snow peas, chilies and half the dressing. Gently combine.

Serve: Divide the remaining tofu onto 4 warmed serving plates, cover with the avocado and mango mixture, top with the snow pea sprouts. Drizzle the plates with the remaining dressing and serve immediately.

Cheesy Filo Parcels

Feta cheese is a white, dry, crumbly cheese that can be made either from cows', ewes' or goats' milk. It is matured in brine to give it a sharp acidic and salty taste. These small triangles of crisp filo pastry with a savoury soft centre contain a mix of feta and haloumi cheese.

makes 16

125g (4½ ounces) *feta* cheese

125g (4½ ounces) *haloumi* cheese

1–2 tablespoons chopped fresh thyme or mint

½ teaspoon freshly-ground black pepper

1 tablespoon caraway seeds, dry-roasted and coarsely ground

12 sheets filo pastry

¼ cup olive oil or melted butter

Preheat the oven to 200°C/ 400°F.

Grate the *feta* and *haloumi* cheese into a bowl and mix in the thyme or mint, the pepper and the roasted caraway seeds.

Cut the stack of filo sheets lengthwise into 3 even strips with a sharp knife. This will give you 36 strips of pastry.

Brush one strip with smears of butter or oil and place a second strip on top. At the base of this, spoon on a small tablespoon of the cheese mixture.

Fold the bottom edge of the pastry up to form a triangle over the filling. Continue to flip the triangle over and over, working up the pastry strip until it is all used up, forming a little triangular parcel.

Repeat this procedure until all the pastry and cheese is used. Place the parcels on a baking sheet and brush with the remaining butter or oil.

Bake in the hot oven for about 15 minutes, or until the parcels are crisp and golden.

Serve the cheesy filo parcels warm or at room temperature.

Pan-fried Haloumi Steaks

Haloumi cheese is a soft to semi-hard cheese made from ewes' or goats' milk with a salty, lactic flavour, and is one of the few cheeses that can be successfully pan-fried. Sizzling fried slabs of haloumi cheese take only minutes to prepare.

serves 4

1 teaspoon butter

250g (9 ounces) *haloumi* cheese, drained and sliced 5mm (¼-inch)

1 lemon

Heat a non-stick pan over moderate heat and melt the butter.

Fry the cheese slices until golden brown on both sides.

Squeeze a little lemon over the cheese.

Serve piping hot with crusty bread.

Note: As an alternative serving suggestion, cook and serve the cheese in small single-serve cast-iron dishes. The cast iron will hold its heat, helping to keep the cheese soft and supple.

Asparagus with Semi-dried Tomato & Macadamia Salsa

makes 4 entrée serves

½ cup macadamias, toasted and coarsely chopped

½ cup semi-dried tomatoes, coarsely chopped

2 tablespoons chopped flat-leaf parsley

1½ tablespoons olive oil

1 tablespoon balsamic vinegar or lemon juice

½ teaspoon salt

½ teaspoon freshly-ground black pepper

2 or 3 bunches asparagus, trimmed

shaved Parmesan, to serve

Combine the macadamia nuts, semi-dried tomato, parsley, oil, vinegar, salt and pepper. Mix well.

Steam the asparagus over boiling water for 1–2 minutes, or until just tender.

Serve the asparagus topped with the tomato mixture and shaved Parmesan.

Note: To steam asparagus, either stand it in a special asparagus cooker, or lay it flat in a wide pan of boiling water and cook it for about 2 minutes — less for thin spears. Carefully lift out the asparagus, refresh it under gently running cold water, and drain it on a folded kitchen towel.

Egyptian Crumbly Spice & Nut Dip (Dukkah)

Different versions of dukkah are found all over the Middle East, and this variation is from Egypt. It's a very personal and individual mixture that varies from one family to another — so no two versions are exactly the same.

makes about 2½ cups

½ cup hazelnuts

¾ cup sesame seeds

½ cup coriander seeds

½ cup cumin seeds

1 teaspoon salt

½ teaspoon pepper

olive oil and crusty bread for serving

Preheat the oven to 180°C/350°F. **Roast** the hazelnuts on an oven tray for about 15 minutes, or until fragrant. Remove them from the oven, and when a little cool, rub away as much of the brown skin from the nuts as you can.

Toast the sesame seeds in a heavy frying pan over moderate heat, stirring often, for about 4 minutes, or until golden brown and aromatic. Empty the toasted seeds into a bowl. Toast the coriander seeds in a similar manner for about 2–3 minutes. Repeat for the cumin, toasting for about 2 minutes.

Pound the seeds and nuts using a mortar and pestle, or whiz them in a spice or coffee grinder. The mixture should be dry and crumbly, not oily. Combine the crushed nuts and seeds with the salt and pepper.

Serve as a dip with olive oil and crusty bread.

Note: The mixture will keep in a sealed container for many weeks.

Dukkah is a loose, coarsely-ground mixture of sesame seeds, hazelnuts, aromatic cumin and coriander. It is delicious eaten on oil-dunked bread for breakfast, or as a snack. *Dukkah* has recently started appearing quite regularly on restaurant menus as an appetizer, hence its inclusion in this chapter.

The important thing to remember about *dukkah* is that it should be dry and crumbly. It is easy to over-grind the ingredients, especially the nuts, which makes the mixture too oily. To prevent this, cool the ingredients after roasting, then proceed slowly.

Polenta is a fine yellow cornmeal, which after cooking into a thick porridge can be cooled and sliced. In this dish, succulent cubes of cheesy polenta are topped with a tasty herbed tomato purée. Colourful finger food!

Baked Cheesy Polenta Squares
with Spicy Tomato Concasse

makes about 40

4 cups water

1 teaspoon salt

1¼ cups polenta

100g (3½ ounces) Parmesan
  cheese

spicy tomato *concasse* (recipe
  follows)

Boil the salted water, whisk in the polenta, and cook, stirring frequently, over low heat for 10 minutes, or until all the liquid is absorbed. Remove from the heat and stir in the Parmesan.

Spoon the polenta into a shallow oiled 25cm x 30cm (10-inch x 12-inch) baking dish, spreading it evenly to a thickness of 1cm. Set aside to cool for 10 minutes.

Bake the polenta in an oven set to the highest temperature until crisp and a little golden on top. Remove, cool and cut into 4cm (1½-inch) squares.

Serve the polenta squares on a tray, topped with heaped teaspoonfuls of spicy tomato *concasse*.

Spicy Tomato Concasse

1 tablespoon olive oil

1 teaspoon grated fresh ginger

1 small red chili, seeded and
  chopped

½ teaspoon yellow asafetida
  powder

2 cups chopped peeled tomatoes

2 tablespoons chopped *kalamata*
  olives, or olives of your choice

1 tablespoon chopped basil leaves

1 teaspoon sugar

½ teaspoon salt

Heat the olive oil in a large heavy-based saucepan, add the ginger and chili, and cook over low heat for a couple of minutes, or until soft. Sprinkle in the asafetida and fry momentarily.

Stir in the tomatoes, bring to the boil then simmer, stirring occasionally, over low heat for 5–10 minutes, or until a little reduced.

Add the chopped olives, basil, sugar and salt, then continue cooking for 5–10 minutes more, or until it becomes a thick purée. Remove from the heat.

Serve with the cheesy polenta squares.

If you double the quantities for this rich appetizer and add a rice dish, as well as a salad or soup, you have a delicious substantial meal.

Creamy Cauliflower &
Snow Peas with Cashews

serves 4

oil or ghee for deep-frying
3 cups cauliflower florets
150g (6 ounces) snow peas
1 teaspoon olive oil
¼ teaspoon yellow asafetida
  powder
½ cup sour cream
½ teaspoon salt
½ teaspoon freshly-ground black
  pepper

½ cup whole roasted unsalted
  cashews
1 teaspoon sweet chili sauce
1 tablespoon chopped fresh
  coriander leaves

Heat oil or ghee for deep-frying in a wok or pan over fairly high heat. When the oil is hot, deep-fry the cauliflower pieces in batches, frying them until they can just be pierced with a knifepoint. Drain the cauliflower pieces, keeping them warm.

Blanch the snow peas in boiling, lightly salted water for 1 minute, or until just tender, and drain them.
Heat 1 teaspoon of olive oil in a frying pan. Sprinkle in the yellow asafetida powder and fry momentarily. Stir-fry the snow peas in the hot oil for 1 minute. Remove from the heat.
Fold in the cauliflower pieces, sour cream, salt, pepper, cashews, sweet chili sauce and coriander leaves.
Serve immediately.

Until I tried them, I doubted that oven-baked 'fried potatoes' could be delicious. But they are — and they're virtually fat-free because they're actually 'fried' in hot air! Crisp on the outside and moist on the inside — just like 'chips' should be, they can be jazzed up with any of the seasonings listed below, or served plain.

Oven-fried Potato Wedges
with Quick Tomato Chutney

makes 6–8 appetizer serves

1 kg (2 pounds) Idaho-type unpeeled baking potatoes, cut into country-style wedges

olive oil spray

1 teaspoon salt, or to taste

any of the following optional seasonings: ½ teaspoon ground cumin; ¼ teaspoon turmeric powder; ¼ teaspoon cayenne; ½ teaspoon sweet paprika (my favourite); ½ teaspoon lemon pepper; ½ teaspoon ground black pepper; ½ teaspoon crushed dried rosemary

tomato chutney (recipe follows)

Preheat the oven to 230°C/450°F. **Place** the potato wedges in a bowl and spray well with oil. Sprinkle with the salt and your choice of seasoning. Toss to mix. Remove a rack from the upper centre of the oven. **Lay** the wedges in a single layer directly on the rack. Carefully return the rack to the oven.

Bake for about 20 minutes, or until the potatoes are tender with a deep golden-brown crust.

Serve piping hot as is, or with a splash of lemon juice, a drizzle of sauce or the accompanying tomato chutney.

Note: If you're using a fan-forced oven, reduce the cooking time by 5 minutes. The hot air circulating around the potatoes cooks them faster.

Quick Tomato Chutney

If you put this on the stove when the potato wedges go in the oven, it'll be ready the same time as they are.

1 tablespoon olive oil or ghee

½ teaspoon brown mustard seeds

1 small green chili, seeded and chopped

1 teaspoon shredded fresh ginger

Heat the oil or ghee in a large, heavy pan over fairly high heat.

Sprinkle in the mustard seeds and fry them until they crackle. Drop in the chili and ginger and fry for one minute or until aromatic.

Add the chopped tomatoes. Cook, stirring often, for about 10 minutes, or until fairly thick and reduced. Stir in the salt and sugar, cook for another couple of minutes, then remove from the heat.

Serve hot, warm or at room temperature. Makes 2 cups.

Corn Raita with Chili Crisps,
Pappadams, & Indonesian Emping Crackers

This cooling yogurt-based raita is studded with succulent corn and swirled with
toasted spices. The trio of accompanying crispies can be whipped up in a few minutes.

serves 6

The raita

2 cups plain yogurt

2 cups sour cream

corn from 2 large ears cooked
   fresh corn, or 2 cups frozen
   corn, thawed

1 teaspoon salt

2 tablespoons ghee or oil

2 teaspoons black mustard seeds

2 teaspoons cumin seeds

½ teaspoon yellow asafetida
   powder

1 tablespoon finely-chopped
   fresh ginger

1 tablespoon finely-chopped
   fresh mint

pinch cayenne pepper

2 tablespoons coarsely-chopped
   fresh coriander leaves

1 hot green chili, seeded and finely
   chopped

The rest of the ingredients

oil for deep-frying

150g (5 ounces) *emping* crackers

12 square egg-free wonton
   wrappers, cut into 2 or 3
   triangles

finely ground salt

chili powder

1 packet *pappadams*, variety and
   size to taste

The raita

Combine the yogurt, sour cream, cooked corn and salt in a medium-sized mixing bowl.

Heat the ghee or oil in a small frying pan over moderate heat. Add the mustard seeds and fry until they start to crackle. Sprinkle in the cumin seeds and toast them until they darken a few shades. Remove the pan from the heat, drop in the yellow asafetida powder, swirl the pan momentarily, then tip the contents of the frying pan into the bowl of corn, yogurt and sour cream.

Stir to incorporate the spices, then fold in the ginger, mint, cayenne, coriander leaves and fresh chili. Mix well, allowing the flavours to blend while you prepare the crispy accompaniments.

The emping crackers

Heat oil in a wok or deep pan to about 180°C/350°F.

Drop in a small handful of *emping* into the hot oil. They will puff up. Stir them continuously for 10–20 seconds or until they have changed colour a little, then remove them with a large slotted spoon, and drain on paper towels. Repeat for all crackers.

Sprinkle with salt while they are still hot.

The chilli crisps

Heat oil to about 180°C/350°F.

Drop in a few triangles of pastry and fry for 10–20 seconds, or until crisp and golden. Drain on paper towels. Repeat for all the crisps.

Sprinkle crisps with chili powder and salt to taste.

The pappadams

Heat oil to 180°C/350°F.

Lower a *pappadam* into the hot oil with tongs. Fry briefly, remove and drain. Repeat for all the *pappadams*. Alternatively toast over an open flame, heat them one at a time under a grill until golden and crisp, or toast them in a microwave.

Serve the zesty corn *raita* with its crispy accompaniments.

Hint: *Emping* keep crisp for 2 weeks if sealed tightly in a jar, and chili crisps stay crisp in an airtight container for 2 days. *Pappadams* are best served as soon as they are cooked.

Indonesian emping crackers are grain-free vegetarian crisps made from *melinjo* nuts that have been shelled, pounded and sundried. They are readily available in well-stocked Asian grocers, and are variously labelled as *melinjo* nut crackers, *emping* or *krupuk emping* (*krupuk* means crackers). Their taste is something like walnuts. The chili crisps are made from wonton pastry, which you'll find in the freezers of Asian grocers.

Soups

Pepper water is the origin of the pukkah old Anglo-Indian hybrid known as Mullitawny. Charmaine Solomon explains: "The name mulligatawny originates from the Tamil language, in which molagu means pepper, and thanni means water. All it contains is a mixture of spices, garlic, tamarind for piquancy, and perhaps a tiny pinch of asafetida which acts as a carminative."

My version contains no garlic, because I don't like it. And asafetida is definitely included because I do like it (just in case you haven't noticed).

Pepper Water

makes 4–6 small appetizer serves

1 tablespoon dried tamarind pulp

1 teaspoon freshly-ground black
  pepper, preferably Malabar

1 teaspoon ground cumin seeds

¼ cup chopped fresh coriander
  leaves

1 teaspoon salt

2 teaspoons mild vegetable oil

1 teaspoon black mustard seeds

1 large sprig fresh curry leaves

½ teaspoon yellow asafetida
  powder

Soak the tamarind in a cup of boiling water for 10 minutes, then squeeze to extract the sour, fruity pulp. Strain, discarding the seeds and fibre.

Combine the tamarind liquid, pepper, cumin, coriander leaves and salt, with 1 litre/quart cold water in a saucepan over full heat.

Bring to the boil, reduce the heat and simmer for 10 minutes.

Prepare the final seasonings as follows: Heat the oil in a small saucepan over moderate heat. When the oil is hot, sprinkle in the mustard seeds and fry them until they crackle. Roughly tear the curry leaves and add them to the hot oil – careful – they may crackle violently. When the leaves are withered, sprinkle in the asafetida powder, sauté momentarily.

Pour the spices into the simmering pepper water.

Serve immediately to either sip with the meal, or serve after the meal as a digestive.

Urad dal lentils are a great favourite all over the Indian sub-continent.
This is a country-style, semi-dry dal side dish that fits especially well into a
meal that includes flat breads.

Fennel-laced Urad Dal

serves 4

1 ½ cups split *urad dal*, soaked in
    water for 1 hour, drained and
    rinsed

5 cups water

2 green chilies, seeded and minced

1 tablespoon minced fresh ginger

2 tablespoons ghee

1 ½ teaspoons cumin seeds

1 ½ teaspoons fennel seeds

½ teaspoon yellow asafetida
    powder

1 teaspoon salt

1 tablespoon chopped fresh
    coriander leaves

Combine the soaked and drained *dal*, the water, chili and ginger in a medium saucepan and bring to the boil over moderate heat.

Cook, partially covered, for 25 minutes, or until the *dal* is soft and broken. For even better results, cook in a pressure cooker.

Season as follows: heat the ghee in a small saucepan or frying pan over moderate heat. When the ghee is fairly hot, drop in the cumin and fennel seeds. When they darken a few shades, sprinkle in the yellow asafetida powder, fry momentarily, then pour the whole ghee and spice mixture into the simmering *dal*. Add the salt.

Serve hot in warmed soup bowls garnished with a sprinkle of the chopped fresh coriander leaves.

In Thai cuisine, most soups are served as a side dish as part of a full meal. They are meant to be light and refreshing to counter-balance heavier, richer dishes. My vegetarian version of the well-known Tom Yum is full of bold, strong flavours like coriander roots, lemongrass, chili, kaffir lime leaves and the sour, spinach-like vegetable sorrel.

Hot & Sour Tom Yum Soup

serves 6

4 scraped coriander roots

4 sticks lemongrass, white parts only

1 teaspoon yellow asafetida powder

2 or 3 small fresh hot red chilies, chopped

2 litres/quarts rich vegetable stock (recipe follows)

4 *kaffir* lime leaves

4 large ripe tomatoes, blanched, peeled and coarsely chopped

400g (13 ounces) firm pressed tofu, cut into 2.5cm (1-inch) pieces

1 bunch sorrel, torn

2 or 3 small fresh hot red chilies, extra, sliced diagonally

5 tablespoons soy sauce

½ cup lime juice

2/3 cup chopped fresh coriander leaves

Pound the coriander roots, lemongrass, asafetida and chili to a rough paste using a mortar and pestle. Alternatively, process in a blender with a few drops of water.

Boil the vegetable stock in a saucepan over full heat. Drop in the *kaffir* lime leaves and tomato and cook for 2 or 3 minutes.

Add the spice paste, reduce the heat to a simmer, add the tofu and sorrel and cook for another 2 minutes.

Serve: Divide the extra chili, the soy sauce, lime juice and chopped coriander into large deep serving bowls and pour the boiling soup over. Serve with hot steamed rice.

Vegetable Stock

This is a basic Vietnamese vegetable stock known as *nuoc leo raucai*. I use it as a basis for many Asian soups.

4 litres/quarts water

1 cup carrots, sliced

1 cup cabbage, sliced

½ cup celery stalk, sliced

I cup white radish, sliced

1½ teaspoons salt

Combine all the ingredients in a saucepan and boil for 1 hour, or until the liquid has reduced by half.

Strain and set aside.

The French borrowed pesto, the paste of ground basil, olive oil, cheese and pine nuts from their Italian neighbours, adapted it to suit their own taste, and called it pistou. I've seen many different versions of this famous French soup. The essential ingredient that sets it apart from minestrone is the basil paste, which gives the soup its name and individuality.

La Soupe au Pistou

makes 4 hearty serves

1 tablespoon olive oil

1 teaspoon yellow asafetida powder

2 skinned and chopped tomatoes, or
  1 cup tomato purée

1 litre/quart water

2 teaspoons salt

½ teaspoon black pepper

1 cup green beans cut into 2cm
  (¼-inch) lengths

1 medium zucchini, diced

2 or 3 potatoes, diced

½ cup celery leaves

¾ cup cooked white haricot beans

60g (2 ounces) wheat vermicelli,
  broken into 2cm (1-inch) lengths

1½ packed cups fresh basil leaves

2 or 3 tablespoons extra virgin
  olive oil

grated Parmesan cheese to serve

Heat the olive oil in a medium-sized saucepan over moderate heat. When slightly hot, sprinkle in the yellow asafetida powder. Sauté momentarily.

Add the tomatoes, raise the heat and cook them, stirring occasionally, for 10 minutes or until broken down and pulpy. Pour in the water, and add the salt, pepper, green beans, zucchini, potato and celery leaves. Bring to the boil and allow to cook over a vigorous heat for 10–15 minutes, or until the vegetables are soft.

Stir in the cooked haricot beans and the vermicelli, reduce the heat to a simmer, and cook for 5 minutes more, or until the vermicelli is soft.

Make the *pistou* as follows: Pound the basil leaves with a large mortar and pestle, and gradually incorporate the olive oil. Alternatively, process the basil in a food processor, add the olive oil, then process to a smooth paste.

Serve: Combine the *pistou* with the soup just before serving, off the heat, and ladle into warmed bowls. Alternatively, swirl a tablespoon of *pistou* on each individual bowl of soup. Serve the Parmesan in a separate bowl for diners to sprinkle.

The grain product of North African fame couscous is added at the end of the cooking to enrich and thicken this hearty Moroccan-flavoured soup.

Couscous and Vegetable Soup

serves 6

2 tablespoons olive oil

½ teaspoon yellow asafetida

2 medium potatoes, chopped

1 carrot, peeled and chopped

½ small cinnamon stick

¼ teaspoon ground cardamom

1 teaspoon sweet paprika

¼ teaspoon chili powder

2 litres/quarts vegetable stock

2 cups chopped tomatoes

2 tablespoons tomato paste

1 teaspoon salt

½ teaspoon freshly-ground black pepper

1 zucchini, chopped

4 small yellow button squashes, quartered

½ cup *couscous*

2 tablespoons chopped fresh coriander leaves

Heat the olive oil in a large saucepan over moderate heat. Sprinkle in the yellow asafetida powder, stir briefly, add the potatoes and carrots and sauté them in the flavoured oil for 2 or 3 minutes.

Drop in the cinnamon, cardamom, paprika and chili powder, pour in the stock, and add the tomatoes, tomato paste, salt and pepper.

Simmer, partially covered for about 15 minutes, or until the vegetables soften. Add the zucchini and squash and cook for a further 5–10 minutes, or until they are just tender.

Whisk in the *couscous* and cook, stirring occasionally, for an additional 5 minutes.

Serve in warm soup bowls with a sprinkle of fresh coriander.

In Morocco, Harira features prominently on the menu during the Muslim month of Ramadan, where it is consumed with great gusto every night to break the fast. My vegetarian version is redolent with pepper and saffron, and is made meaty with the addition of chewy chunks of shallow-fried tempe, an easily digestible, high protein soy product. You may prefer to add small chunks of fried panir cheese instead.

Moroccan Bean & Vegetable Soup (Harira)

6 hearty serves

3 litres/quarts water
250g (9 ounces) brown lentils
250g (9 ounces) cooked chickpeas
2 tablespoons olive oil
1 teaspoon yellow asafetida
  powder
600ml (1 pint) tomato purée
250g (9 ounces) *tempe*, cubed and
  shallow-fried in hot oil until
  golden brown
1 teaspoon ginger powder
½ teaspoon saffron threads,
  ground and soaked in 2
  tablespoons water
1 bunch continental parsley
1 bunch fresh coriander
100g (3½ ounces) wheat
  vermicelli, broken into
  small pieces
2 teaspoons salt
1½ teaspoons black pepper
juice from 1 large lemon

Boil the water in a large saucepan over full heat. Add the lentils, reduce the heat and simmer for 10 minutes or until half cooked. Add the cooked chickpeas, and simmer for another 10 minutes or until the lentils are soft but not broken.

Heat the oil in a small pan over moderate heat, and when slightly hot, sprinkle in the yellow asafetida powder. Pour into the soup.

Add the tomato purée, chunks of fried *tempe*, the ginger, saffron infusion, half the herbs and the vermicelli. Return the soup to a rolling boil and cook the soup for 10 minutes more, or until the noodles are tender. Finally add the salt, pepper, the remaining herbs, and the lemon juice.

Serve hot with rice, *couscous,* or bread.

Note: Instead of adding *tempe* to the soup, add cubed and pan-fried *panir* cheese made from 2 litres/quarts milk.

Jaipur, the famed Pink City in Rajasthan, India, houses several remarkable palaces. In the emormous City Palace — literally a small city within a city — is the present home of the Maharaja of Jaipur. In the centre of the compound, surrounded by gardens, sits the spectacular Sri Radha Govinda Temple. I fondly remember my visits to Jaipur, stunning architecture, dedicated residents and its delicious vegetarian cuisine.

Jaipur-style Quick & Easy Mung Dal

serves 6

1 cup split mung beans, soaked in
  water for 1 hour, rinsed and
  drained

7 cups water

½ teaspoon turmeric powder

1 cup carrots, diced

2 cups small cauliflower florets

2 tablespoons ghee

2 tablespoons cumin seeds

½ teaspoon fennel seeds

1 or 2 green chilies, seeded and
  chopped

1 tablespoon chopped fresh ginger

¼ cup chopped fresh coriander
  leaves

2 tablespoons fresh lemon juice

1 teaspoon salt

¼ teaspoon black pepper

Combine the mung *dal*, water, turmeric and carrots in a heavy, medium-sized saucepan over full heat and bring to the boil. Reduce the heat and simmer, semi-covered, for 15 minutes, or until the *dal* starts to break down.

Add the cauliflower and cook 10 minutes more.

Season as follows: Heat the ghee in a small saucepan over moderate heat. Sprinkle in the cumin and fennel seeds and fry them until they darken a few shades. Add the chilies and ginger and fry until aromatic.

Pour the contents of the whole saucepan into the simmering soup. Add the fresh coriander leaves, lemon juice, salt and pepper.

Serve hot in warmed soup bowls with rice or bread.

The sweet, rustic licorice taste of fennel is at once unmistakable and subtle. It is so flavourful that it requires no stock, only water, and no extra herbs to transform it into a full-bodied hearty, satisfying soup. If the inner core of the fennel is tough and stringy, remove it with a paring knife.

Cream of Fennel Soup

serves 6

4 tablespoons unsalted butter

1 teaspoon yellow asafetida powder

4 medium fennel bulbs, thinly sliced

1 large red potato, sliced

6½ cups cold water

1 cup heavy cream

2 teaspoons salt

½ teaspoon freshly-ground black pepper

2 tablespoons chopped fennel greens

Melt the butter in a large saucepan over moderate heat. Sprinkle in the yellow asafetida powder and sauté momentarily.

Stir in the sliced fennel and fry, stirring occasionally, until slightly tender and translucent.

Add the sliced potato, cold water, cream, salt and pepper. Bring to the boil, then cover with a lid, reduce the heat and simmer for 20 minutes, or until the fennel is soft and tender.

Purée the soup using a food processor, blender or hand-held mixer.

Pour the soup through a fine strainer.

Serve: Stir in the chopped fennel greens, then ladle into 6 warm soup bowls.

Creamy coconut milk, tart lime juice and spicy red curry paste blend beautifully with the mildness of the sweet potatoes. The bold colour of pink-fleshed sweet potatoes complete the sensory experience.

Thai-flavoured Sweet Potato Soup

serves 6

750g (1½ pounds) pink-fleshed
   sweet potatoes, peeled and sliced
6 cups rich vegetable stock
2 tablespoons olive oil
1 teaspoon yellow asafetida
   powder
400ml (13 fluid ounces)
   coconut milk
¼ cup fresh lime juice
2 teaspoons red curry paste (recipe
   follows)
1½ teaspoons salt
½ teaspoon black pepper
½ cup coriander leaves for garnish

Boil the sweet potatoes in lightly salted water for about 20 minutes or until tender. Remove the sweet potatoes from their cooking water, set the cooking water aside, and rinse and dry the saucepan.

Process the sweet potatoes in a food processor or blender with sufficient rich vegetable stock to make a smooth purée.

Warm the oil in the saucepan over moderate heat, sprinkle in the yellow asafetida powder and sauté briefly.

Pour in the sweet potato purée. Add the rest of the rich vegetable stock, the coconut milk, lime juice, red curry paste, salt and pepper. If the soup is too thick, add some reserved cooking liquid. Warm through until almost boiling.

Serve: Ladle the soup into warm soup bowls and serve hot with a garnish of fresh coriander leaves.

Red Curry Paste

7 dried red chilies
2 teaspoons coriander seeds
2 teaspoons chopped *galangal*
2 teaspoons chopped lemongrass
1 tablespoon *kaffir* lime peel
1 teaspoon yellow asafetida
   powder
1 teaspoon salt

Pound together the dried chilies and coriander seeds in a stone mortar until completely pulverised.

Add the *galangal,* grind to a paste, then add and grind the lemongrass, then the *kaffir* lime peel, asafetida and salt. Use the required quantity in the soup, and refrigerate the remainder until needed.

As the name suggests, this is a quick-to-prepare dish, a heart-warming combination of briefly cooked Ratatouille-style vegetables simmered in a light broth and infused with Asian flavours. Try it with rice, or with chunks of fresh crusty bread. Trés bonza!

Quick Ratatouille Soup

serves 6

2 tablespoons olive oil

1 teaspoon grated fresh ginger

1 celery stalk, diced 1.5cm (½ inch)

6 large ripe tomatoes, peeled
  seeded and chopped

1 medium zucchini, diced 1.5cm
  (½ inch)

1 medium red capsicum (pepper),
  diced 1.5cm (½ inch)

2½ cups vegetable stock

2½ cups tomato juice

2 tablespoons fresh coriander
  leaves, chopped

1 teaspoon salt

¼ teaspoon cayenne pepper,
  optional

1–2 teaspoons sugar, optional

1 teaspoon cumin seeds, pan-
  toasted until golden and crushed

Warm the oil in a heavy saucepan over moderate heat. Stir in the ginger, celery, tomato, zucchini and capsicum.

Cook, stirring occasionally, for 10 minutes. Add the stock and tomato juice and simmer for a further 10 minutes. Stir in the coriander, salt, and optional cayenne and sugar.

Serve: Ladle into bowls and sprinkle with the crushed cumin.

This is a quick, tasty soup eaten in the coastal regions of Western India.

Marathi Spinach Soup (Palak Saar)

serves 4

- 2 tablespoons ghee
- 1 teaspoon brown mustard seeds
- 1 small dried red chili
- 2 *tej patta* leaves, or bay leaves
- 1 small green chili, seeded and finely chopped
- 1 tablespoon fresh ginger, finely-minced
- 1 teaspoon yellow asafetida powder
- 1 bunch spinach, about 300g (10 ounces), stalks removed, washed and finely-sliced
- 2 tablespoons plain flour mixed with 1 cup cold water to form a paste
- 300ml (½ pint) coconut milk
- 1 teaspoon salt

Heat the ghee in a medium saucepan over moderate heat. When fairly hot, sprinkle in the mustard seeds and fry until they crackle. Add the dried red chili and the bay leaves, and sauté until they darken in colour.
Add the minced fresh chili and ginger, and fry until aromatic. Sprinkle in the asafetida, add the spinach, and fry for 2 or 3 minutes, or until the spinach wilts and softens.

Add the flour and water paste to the softened spinach, followed quickly with the coconut milk plus 1 cup hot water Add the salt, bring to the boil, reduce the heat and simmer for 10 minutes, or until the spinach is butter-soft and the soup is thick and creamy.

Serve the soup hot with crusty bread or rice.

The avocado is a non-traditional
addition to my version of this traditional
Spanish chilled soup.

Avocado-laced Gazpacho Soup

serves 4–6

4 medium-sized ripe tomatoes,
  chopped

1 red capsicum (pepper), chopped

1 Lebanese cucumber, peeled and
  chopped

2 medium-sized avocados, peeled

750ml (1ı pints) tomato juice

¼ cup lime juice

1 tablespoon chopped flat-leaf
  parsley

1 tablespoon chopped mint

¼ teaspoon yellow asafetida
  powder

1 teaspoon salt

½ teaspoon freshly-ground black
  pepper

2 teaspoons each extra chopped
  parsley and mint for garnish

Pulse the tomato, capsicum, cucumber and one avocado in
a food processor until slightly textured. If necessary, add a
little tomato juice to aid in the blending.

Pour the mixture into a large serving bowl, stir in the tomato
juice, lime juice, parsley, mint, asafetida powder, salt and pepper. Mix well.

Chop the remaining avocado into tiny pieces.

Serve: Ladle the soup into 6 serving bowls and top each with
some chopped avocado and a light sprinkle of the reserved
chopped herbs.

Vegetable
Dishes

There are three Middle Eastern rice varieties in this chapter, starting with a Syrian way, cooked using the absorption method and adorned simply with butter. Be sure to use a pot with a very tight-fitting lid, since steaming is employed in this recipe, or else use extra water.

Syrian-style Rice

serves 4–6

2 cups long grain rice, preferably
   basmati
2¼ to 2½ cups water
½ teaspoon salt
3 tablespoons butter

Wash the rice: Boil 4 cups water and pour over the rice in a large bowl. Stir well for a few seconds, pour the rice through a sieve or a small-holed colander and rinse under cold running water until the water runs clear. Drain the rice well.

Combine the water and salt in a small saucepan and bring it to boil over moderate heat.

Pour in the rice and stir until it returns to the boil. Boil vigorously for 30 seconds, then place the rice over your lowest heat source, cover the pan with a very tight-fitting lid, and simmer very gently for 20 minutes without removing the lid so as to allow a build-up of steam. When the time is up, the rice should be tender and separate, with little holes all over the surface.

Remove the rice from the heat, and set it aside for another 5 minutes to allow the delicate rice grains to firm up. Just before serving, melt the butter and pour it over the rice.

Serve hot.

The subject of rice cooking is at once fascinating, vast, and variegated, and can only just be touched on in this book. There are two basic methods of cooking rice: one consists of boiling it in plenty of water and then draining, and the other of cooking it in a precisely measured amount of water which becomes completely absorbed by the rice. Both methods give individual and fluffy grains of rice, both can be spiced or unspiced, and both take around the same amount of time to cook.

When rice is boiled in a large amount of water, the grains swell to a somewhat larger size and are slightly softer. I find that rice cooked by the absorption method has marginally more flavour and has a more *al dente* texture.

Apart from the North African group of countries—Morocco, Algeria and Tunisia—who prefer *couscous* as their staple grain, Middle Eastern countries have a great tradition of rice cooking. It is usually enhanced by butter, or ghee (clarified butter) known as *smen* or *sammneh* (depending on which part of the Middle East you live in). Rice is cooked slightly differently from Middle Eastern country to country.

Arab-style Rice with Vermicelli & Chickpeas

I have added chickpeas to this everyday Arab rice dish and transformed it into something very delicious. Served with a crisp green salad and some fresh yogurt, you've made yourself a delicious lunch or dinner.

serves 4–6

3 cups water

1 teaspoon salt

1 tablespoon butter

1 tablespoon olive oil

100g (3 ounces) wheat vermicelli, about ¾ cup, broken into short pieces

1 teaspoon yellow asafetida

1½ cups long-grain rice, such as basmati

1¼ cups cooked chickpeas

Boil the water and salt in a small saucepan over moderate heat. Reduce the heat to low, and cover with a lid.

Heat the butter and oil together in a larger saucepan over moderate heat. When hot, drop in the vermicelli and stir-fry until golden brown. Sprinkle in the yellow asafetida powder, followed by the rice, and sauté the grains for 1 minute or until well-coated in oil.

Pour in the boiling water, allow the rice to come to the boil, reduce the heat to low, cover with a tight-fitting lid and gently simmer, without stirring, for 10 minutes.

Remove the lid briefly after 10 minutes and drop in the cooked chickpeas. Quickly replace the lid and continue cooking the rice for another 10 minutes or until the grains are soft and fluffy, and all the liquid has been absorbed. Set the rice aside for 5 minutes to firm up.

Serve hot with a crisp green salad and yogurt.

Basmati rice is the famous light-textured, long-grained aromatic rice from North India and Pakistan. It has a wonderful fragrance and flavour, even just served plain. Basmati rice is easy to cook, and although more costly than other long-grained rice, it is well worth the extra expense. This rice dish, studded with crisp toasted cashews, green peas and fresh coriander leaves is an ideal dish to make for a party or a special luncheon.

Basmati Rice with Cashews,
Peas & Fresh Coriander

serves 4–6

2 ¾ cups water

1 ½ teaspoons salt

½ teaspoon turmeric

2 tablespoons ghee
  or olive oil

½ teaspoon yellow asafetida
  powder

1 ½ cups *basmati* rice

1 cup peas

1 cup toasted cashews

¼ cup chopped
  coriander leaves

extra coriander leaves for garnish

Bring to a boil the water, salt and turmeric in a small saucepan over moderate heat. Cover tightly and reduce to a simmer.

Heat the ghee or oil in another, larger saucepan over moderate heat. Sprinkle in the yellow asafetida powder, stir briefly, add the rice and sauté for about 2 minutes, or until the rice turns a little whitish in colour.

Pour the simmering water into the rice, stir briefly, and if using fresh peas add them now. Increase the heat, return the rice to a full boil, reduce the heat to very low and cover with a tight-fitting lid.

Simmer the rice for 15–20 minutes or until all the water is absorbed and the rice is tender and flaky. If using thawed frozen peas, lift the lid 5 minutes before the end and toss the peas in, quickly replacing the lid.

Remove from the heat, leaving it covered and undisturbed for 5 minutes to allow the tender grains to firm up.

Fold in the cashews and chopped coriander leaves.

Serve hot, garnished with the remaining herbs.

In a traditional Mexican afternoon meal, a sopa seca, known with levity as a 'dry soup'- comes after the 'wet soup' and before the main course. This chili-hot moist rice looks great served in individual ovenproof earthenware ramekins, warmed through in the oven with the cheese melted on top and garnished with a sprig of fresh coriander.

Mexican Rice with Cheese (Sopa de Chapultepec)

serves 6

3 large dried New Mexico chilies

1 medium red capsicum (pepper), roasted in the oven and peeled

2 or 3 tomatillos, husked, or small green tomatoes

1 tablespoon butter

1 tablespoon olive oil

1 teaspoon yellow asafetida powder

1 teaspoon Spanish-style smoked hot paprika powder

2 teaspoons salt

½ teaspoon black pepper

4 cups cooked white rice

300g (10 ounces) cheddar cheese, about 3 cups, grated

2 cups heavy sour cream

handful fresh coriander for garnish

Soak the dried chilis in ½ cup boiling water for 10 minutes.

Pour the chilis and their soaking water into a blender or food processor along with the roasted capsicum and tomatillos. Blend until puréed.

Melt the butter with the oil in a heavy frying pan over moderate heat. Sprinkle in the yellow asafetida powder, sauté momentarily, pour in the blended chili mixture, sprinkle in the smoked paprika, salt and pepper, bring to the boil and cook for 2 or 3 minutes.

Preheat the oven to 180° C/350°F.

Combine the cooked rice, the chili mixture, 1½ cups of the grated cheese and the sour cream in a large bowl.

Spoon the mixture into 6 large earthenware ramekins and top with the remaining cheese.

Bake for about 15 minutes or until heated through, covered loosely with foil for the last 5 minutes.

Serve hot, garnished with fresh coriander leaves.

Note: As an alternative to individual ramekins, bake the rice in a large baking dish.

Sushi refers to cooked short-grain rice mixed with a sweetened vinegar dressing. It can be topped with a number of vegetarian ingredients or rolled with different fillings in dark green nori seaweed — the varieties are enormous (see bara-zushi and inari — zushi). As with any rice, it can be successfully cooked in a saucepan or in an electric rice cooker. Any variety of short grain rice will do, although Japanese varieties are particularly appropriate.

Japanese Sushi Rice

makes about 8 cups

5 cups short-grain rice, a little
   more than 1 kilo (2 pounds)
5 cups water
one 2.5cm (1-inch) square *kombu*,
   dried kelp (optional)

dressing
5 tablespoons *sushi* vinegar
2 tablespoons fine sugar
1 teaspoon salt

Wash and drain the rice.

Place the drained rice and the water, plus the optional *kombu*, in a heavy bottomed saucepan over moderate heat. Stir until the water boils, reduce to a simmer, cover with a tight-fitting lid and cook over a very low heat for 15 minutes, or until the rice is cooked and there is no water remaining in the saucepan.

Remove from the heat. Leave the lid on for an additional 10 minutes to allow the rice to firm up. Remove the *kombu*. Alternatively, place the rice, water and optional *kombu* in an electric rice cooker, and cook according to manufacturer's instructions.

Prepare the vinegar dressing: Place the vinegar, salt and sugar in a non-reactive saucepan and heat while stirring gently over low heat until the sugar and salt dissolve. Do not boil.

Spread the hot rice out evenly in a large, preferably non-metallic, flat-bottomed bowl using a paddle or a wooden spoon.

Pour in the dressing slowly with one hand, gently combining it with the rice while simultaneously fanning the grains with a fan or some newspaper in the other hand. Your aim is to make the rice slightly sticky, with the grains separated and evenly flavoured with the dressing. Continue mixing and fanning until the rice reaches body temperature.

Cover the bowl with a damp cloth. The rice is now ready to be made into *sushi*.

Note: Fanning the rice while mixing in the dressing helps lessen the sourness of the vinegar, adds a glisten to the rice and prevents it from becoming too sticky. Do not refrigerate *sushi* rice or else it will become hard. *Sushi* rice will not keep for more than one day.

Whereas making sushi-nori rolls is not for the novice, bara-zushi is a great one-dish sushi meal that can be made at home. In Japan it is regarded as an everyday meal. Bara-zushi is a tasty melange of seasoned vegetables, crumbled sheets of dried seaweed (nori), strips of deep-fried tofu and traditional sushi rice all served together in a bowl.

Sushi Rice with Vegetables (Bara-zushi)

serves 6

100g (3½ ounces) green beans, bias sliced 2cm (¾-inch)

150g (5 ounces) carrot, julienned

100g (3½ ounces) snow peas, sliced lengthwise

100g (3½ ounces) red capsicum (peppers), diced

150g (5 ounces) cooked baby corn

4 thin deep-fried tofu pouches *(abura-age-dofu)*, sliced into thin strips

3 tablespoons soy sauce

5 cups cooked, cooled and seasoned *sushi* rice (see previous recipe)

2 sheets dried *nori* seaweed, sliced or crumbled

¼ cup pickled ginger

one small avocado, sliced into small pieces

Bring to a boil a few cups of water in a small saucepan over moderate heat. Add the beans and the julienne carrots and simmer for 1–2 minutes, or until the beans are cooked *al dente*. Add the snow peas and capsicum and blanch briefly for 1 minute.

Remove the vegetables with a slotted spoon, rinse under cold running water and drain.

Mix the cooked and drained vegetables, the baby corn, the fried tofu strips and the soy sauce together in a large serving bowl.

Fold in the cooked rice, the crumbled or sliced *nori* seaweed sheets, the pickled ginger and the avocado.

Serve the rice at room temperature.

Note: Instead of folding all the vegetables, sliced tofu and *nori* through the rice, reserve a little of each to garnish the *bara-sushi*. Alternatively, instead of folding any ingredients through the *sushi* rice, decoratively layer all of them on top. The dish is then known as *chirashi-zushi*. *Chirashi* literally means 'scattered'. By the way, *sushi* is pronounced *zushi* when it follows a vowel.

Risotto is one of my favourite ways of eating rice. I love its firm, slightly sticky feel in my mouth, and its wonderful buttery opulence. Spinach looks very appealing in risotto and tastes good too. Please excuse me for sneaking this recipe into the book – it's not that quick a dish to cook, but it's worth the extra few minutes.

Spinach Risotto

serves 6

6–7 cups light vegetable stock

250g (9 ounces) spinach leaves

3 tablespoons butter

½ teaspoon yellow asafetida powder

2 cups *arborio* rice

1 teaspoon salt

big pinch nutmeg

1 cup freshly-grated Parmesan cheese

3 tablespoons extra Parmesan reserved for sprinkling

Bring to a boil the vegetable stock in a medium-sized saucepan over full heat. Add the spinach leaves and blanch for 1 minute. Lower the heat under the stock. Remove the spinach with a slotted spoon. Squeeze out the water from the spinach, returning the water to the simmering stock.

Finely chop the spinach and set it aside.

Melt 2 tablespoons of the butter in a large heavy saucepan over a fairly low heat. Sprinkle in the yellow asafetida powder, stir momentarily, and add the rice.

Stir the rice in the flavoured butter for 1 or 2 minutes to coat it.

Ladle in ½ cup simmering stock. Gently stir the rice and stock. When the stock is absorbed, add another ½ cup. When half the stock has been used, add the spinach to the rice. Continue adding stock and gently stirring the rice until there is no more stock to add. The finished rice should be creamy in texture, and neither soupy nor dry.

Fold the salt, nutmeg, the remaining butter and the Parmesan cheese into the rice and stir through.

Serve the risotto with a garnish of reserved Parmesan cheese.

The lime flavour in this rice dish comes from kaffir lime leaves, the strongly aromatic double-lobed leaves from the tree Citrus histrix. The tree is also sometimes known as the makrut lime. Serve this rice as an accompaniment to a bold-flavoured main course.

Aromatic Lime-scented Rice

serves 4

1½ cups Thai rice

4 *kaffir* lime leaves

3 cups light vegetable stock

1 teaspoon salt

Rinse the rice in a sieve under running water until the water runs clear. Drain well.

Combine the rice, lime leaves, vegetable stock and salt in a medium-sized saucepan. Stirring constantly, bring to the boil over full heat. Reduce to a simmer, cover with a tight-fitting lid and cook over low heat for 15 to 20 minutes, or until the liquid is absorbed and the rice is tender.

Remove from the heat. Allow the rice to stand covered for an additional 5 minutes for the fragile rice grains to firm up. Remove the lime leaves.

Serve hot.

This quick, aromatic rice dish inspired by India's Moghul cuisine is flavoured with both whole and ground cumin, and is made even more aromatic with the addition of cloves and cinnamon. The sweet addition of raisins in a savoury dish is typical of Moghul taste. Based on a recipe by Joyce Westrip from her book Moghul Cooking.

Cumin-flavoured Rice (Jeera Pulao)

serves 4–6

2 ¾ cups water

2 teaspoons salt

2 tablespoons ghee

1 teaspoon cumin seeds

6 whole cloves

one 5cm (2-inch) cinnamon stick

2 teaspoons finely-chopped fresh ginger

1 ½ teaspoons yellow asafetida powder

2 teaspoons ground cumin

3 tablespoons raisins

1 ½ cups *basmati* rice

3 tablespoons lightly cooked fresh peas, or thawed frozen peas

Bring to a boil the water and salt in a small saucepan over moderate heat. Cover with a tight-fitting lid and reduce the heat to low.

Heat the ghee in another, larger saucepan over moderate heat. Add the cumin seeds, cloves and cinnamon stick and toast them until the cumin darkens a few shades. Add the ginger, stir-fry until aromatic, then sprinkle in the asafetida powder, cumin powder, raisins and rice. Stir the rice for 2 minutes or until it turns a little whitish in colour.

Pour in the water, raise the heat and quickly bring the rice to a full boil. Stir briefly then reduce the heat to very low, cover with a tight-fitting lid, and gently simmer without stirring for about 20 minutes, or until the grains are tender.

Lift the lid, drop in the peas, and quickly replace the lid. Remove the rice from the heat and set it aside for 5 minutes to allow the rice grains to firm up. Before serving, remove the cinnamon stick and gently fold in the peas.

Serve piping hot.

The Iranian dish pollou or pillau (from pollo, rice) is a tasty combination of the famous long, narrow-grained fragrant basmati rice cooked by absorption with spices and smen, clarified butter or ghee. This dish was taken to India, where it became pullao, one of the most important rice dishes of the sub-continent. Westwards, this renowned Persian dish became the basis of pilav or pilaf in Turkey and Armenia, the pilafi dishes of Greece and the paellas of Spain.

Iranian Spicy Rice with Saffron *(Pollou)*

serves 4

2½ cups water

1 teaspoon salt

¼ teaspoon saffron threads, ground

4 tablespoons ghee or clarified butter

4 green cardamom pods

4 whole cloves

½ teaspoon cumin seeds

¼ teaspoon black cumin seeds

¼ teaspoon fennel seeds

one 5cm (2-inch) piece cassia bark or cinnamon stick

1½ cups *basmati* rice

Bring to a boil the water, salt and saffron in a saucepan with a tight-fitting lid, and reduce to a simmer.

Heat the ghee in another, larger saucepan over moderate heat.

Stir in the cardamom pods, cloves, the two varieties of cumin, the fennel and cassia, and fry the spices for a couple of minutes, or until they darken a few shades and become aromatic.

Add the rice, and gently stir-fry it for two minutes, or until the grains turn a little whitish in colour.

Pour the simmering water into the toasted grains, increase the heat, and bring to the boil. Reduce the heat to low, cover with a tight-fitting lid and gently simmer, without stirring or lifting the lid, for 20 minutes, or until the water is fully absorbed and the rice is tender.

Remove the rice from the heat, and let it sit, covered, for another 5 minutes to allow the fragile grains to firm up.

Serve piping hot.

Caribbean cooks often tinge their cooking with achiote, the brick-red seeds of the annato tree, Bixa orellana.

Caribbean Yellow Rice (Arroz Amarillo con Achiote)

serves 4-6

2 ¾ cups vegetable stock

1 ½ teaspoons salt

½ teaspoon black pepper

2 tablespoons olive oil

2 teaspoons *annato* seeds

½ teaspoon yellow asafetida powder

1 ½ cups long grain rice

Bring to a boil the stock, salt and pepper in a small saucepan over moderate heat. Reduce the heat to a simmer and cover with a lid.

Heat the oil in a heavy saucepan over low heat. Add the *annato* seeds and fry briefly until the seeds darken and the oil turns a deep reddish-orange. Remove the pan from the heat. Extract the seeds from the oil with a slotted spoon and discard. Return the saucepan to the heat.

Sprinkle the yellow asafetida powder into the coloured oil, sauté momentarily, then add the rice, and gently stir-fry it for 2 minutes, or until the rice goes a little opaque.

Pour the simmering liquid into the sautéed rice. Raise the heat, bring to the boil, then reduce to a simmer. Cover tightly with a lid and cook for 20 minutes, or until the liquid is fully absorbed and the rice is tender and fluffy.

Remove the rice from the heat and let it sit, covered, for another 5 minutes to allow the tender rice grains to firm up.

Serve the rice hot.

Annato oil is used primarily for colour, and has little if any discernible flavour of its own, although I have heard it described as having an 'earthy' flavour. *Annato* does, however, seem to give an enriching roundness to the flavour of the oil.

Caribe Indians used to apply the colour derived from *annato* seeds for body paint. In the dairy industry, *annato* is employed to add an orange hue to some cheeses, notably Red Leicester. Purchase *annato* seeds at specialty shops, Asian or Philippine suppliers.

Rice
Dishes

Chinese broccoli, with its dark green leaves, white flowers and crunchy stalk is also known as gai lan. It is a much-used vegetable in Southern Chinese cuisine. I find the stalks the most delicious part. If gai lan is unavailable from the markets, replace with asparagus or ordinary broccoli.

Chinese Broccoli, Water Chestnuts & Fried Bean Curd

serves 4

1 tablespoon vegetarian oyster sauce

1 tablespoon soy sauce

¼ teaspoon ground white pepper

2 teaspoons sugar

½ cup rich vegetable stock

1 bunch *gai lan*, about 400g (13 ounces), washed and sliced into 8cm (3-inch) lengths

1 tablespoon oil

2cm (¾-inch) chunk of ginger, sliced into wide wafer-thin rounds

½ cup sliced water chestnuts

½ teaspoon yellow asafetida

150g (5 ounces) fried bean curd

Whisk together the vegetarian oyster sauce, soy sauce, white pepper, sugar and vegetable stock in a small bowl. Set aside.

Plunge the *gai lan* into a large saucepan of rapidly boiling, lightly salted water over full heat. Blanch for one or two minutes then remove and drain in a colander. Refresh under cold water, and drain again.

Heat the oil in a wok over high heat, and when almost smoking drop in the ginger. Fry for 30 seconds, or until aromatic. Add the water chestnuts and yellow asafetida powder, and fry for 1 minute.

Pour in the sauce mixture, bring to a boil, and cook for 2–3 minutes, or until the sauce has reduced somewhat.

Add the fried *tofu* and the *gai lan*, combine well, cover the wok and steam for another 1–2 minutes. Remove from the heat.

Serve immediately with hot steamed rice.

The secret of good mashed potatoes lies in choosing the right variety of potatoes, combined with just the right amount of milk, butter and, in this case, cream. The flavour and colour of saffron is a brilliant addition, both visually and taste-wise.

Saffron Mashed Potatoes

serves 4–6

1 kilo (2 pounds) pink-
   skinned potatoes, such as
   Desiree or Pontiac, peeled
   and cut into thick slices
½ cup milk
½ cup cream
¼ teaspoon saffron
   threads, ground
½ cup unsalted butter, cut
   into pieces
¾–1 teaspoon salt
¼ teaspoon pepper

Boil the potatoes in lightly salted water for 15–20 minutes or until tender.
Drain and put through a food mill (to guarantee an absolutely smooth texture), or mash with an old-fashioned potato masher.
Combine the milk, cream and saffron in a saucepan and simmer until the saffron releases its colour and flavour.
Add the cubes of butter to the mashed potato, stirring with a wooden spoon until well incorporated.
Pour in the boiling saffron milk slowly, stirring and beating constantly. Keep the pot over a gentle heat while you beat. Add extra butter and hot milk if the mixture feels heavy. Add the salt and pepper.
Serve hot.

An opulent dish that showcases the incredible meatiness of fried panir cheese. Serve with plenty of rice or bread to mop up the rich juices.

Eggplant & Panir Cheese in Tomato Sauce

serves 6

ghee for deep-frying

1½ teaspoons black mustard seeds

2 teaspoons minced fresh ginger

½ teaspoon minced fresh green chili

½ teaspoon yellow asafetida powder

2 cups tomato purée

¼ teaspoon turmeric powder

1 teaspoon ground coriander

panir cheese from 2½ litres/quarts milk, pressed and cut into 1.5 cm (½-inch) cubes (recipe follows)

1 large eggplant, cut into 1.5 cm (½-inch) cubes

1 teaspoon *garam masala*

2 teaspoons brown sugar

1½ teaspoons salt

Heat 1 tablespoon of ghee in a large frying pan over moderate heat. When the ghee is hot, sprinkle in the mustard seeds and fry them until they crackle. Add the minced ginger and chilies and fry them until aromatic. Sprinkle in the yellow asafetida powder, sauté briefly, and pour in the tomato purée. Stir in the turmeric powder and ground coriander.

Cook the sauce, stirring occasionally, for 10 minutes or until a little reduced.

Heat ghee for deep-frying in a wok or pan over moderate heat. When fairly hot, deep-fry the cubes of *panir* cheese in batches until they are a light golden brown. Remove the fried *panir* from the ghee, and set it aside to drain.

Deep-fry the cubes of eggplant in batches in the hot ghee until golden brown and tender, and set them aside to drain in a colander lined with paper towels.

Fold the *garam masala*, sugar and salt, the fried *panir* cubes and eggplant into the tomato sauce.

Serve hot, with fluffy rice or crusty bread.

Homemade Curd Cheese (Panir)

2½ litres/quarts fresh milk

1–2 cups yogurt or 2–4 tablespoons lemon juice

Heat the milk to boiling point in a heavy-based saucepan. Gradually stir in three-quarters of the yogurt or lemon juice. The milk should separate into chunky curds, leaving a greenish liquid residue called whey. If not completely separated, add a little more yogurt or lemon juice. Drape a double thickness of cheesecloth over a colander sitting in the sink.

Scoop out the curds with a slotted spoon and place them in the cheesecloth. Pour the whey and whatever curds that remain in the saucepan into the cheesecloth. Gather the ends of the cloth together and hold the bag of curd cheese under cold running water for 30 seconds. Twist the bag tightly to squeeze out extra whey, and return it to the colander.

Press under a heavy weight for 10–15 minutes. Remove the curd cheese from the cloth. Your *panir* is ready.

This is a delicious Thai-inspired curry with an easy homemade curry paste that can be whipped up in a few minutes in a blender. Although the curry paste is green, the curry itself will end up being more of a yellow colour from the turmeric. As with all curries, this one is perfect served with a big batch of steaming hot rice.

Green Curry Vegetables & Fried Tofu

serves 6

750g (1½ pounds) potatoes, peeled and cut into 2.5cm (1-inch) cubes

oil or ghee for deep-frying

2 tablespoons oil

green curry paste (recipe follows)

600ml (1 pint) coconut cream

3 tablespoons lime or lemon juice

375g (¾ pound) fried bean curd (tofu)

500g (1 pound) Chinese cabbage, cut into 5cm (2-inch) squares and steamed or stir-fried until just tender

2 cups green peas (thawed frozen peas or cooked fresh peas)

²/₃ –1 cup rich vegetable stock, heated

¼ cup chopped fresh coriander leaves

Deep-fry the potatoes in the oil or ghee in a wok or deep frying pan until golden brown and tender. Drain and set aside, covered.

Heat 2 tablespoons oil in a heavy saucepan over moderately high heat. Stir in a bit more than half of the curry paste (or more for a spicier curry) and fry it in the hot oil for 2–3 minutes, or until it starts to stick on the bottom.

Add the coconut cream and the lime or lemon juice, and cook for 10–15 minutes, or until the sauce is fairly reduced.

Stir in the fried bean curd and mix well. Heat through for 5 minutes. Mix in the cabbage, cooked green peas and the fried potatoes. Add enough vegetable stock to form a rich gravy. Simmer for a further 5 minutes. The potatoes will soak up a fair amount of juice, so be prepared to add more stock.

Fold in the fresh coriander.

Serve hot with lots of hot rice.

Green Curry Paste

2 small fresh red chilies, sliced

1 teaspoon yellow asafetida powder

1 tablespoon grated fresh ginger

½ teaspoon black peppercorns, ground

2 teaspoons ground cumin

1 tablespoon ground coriander

2 teaspoons chopped coriander root

2 tablespoons chopped coriander leaves

2 teaspoons sweet paprika powder

1 teaspoon ground turmeric

2 tablespoons grated dark palm sugar

Process all the ingredients in a blender to form a smooth, green paste. If necessary add a few teaspoons water. You'll need a bit more than half of this paste for the curry. Spoon the remaining curry paste into a clean, screw-top jar and refrigerate for up to three weeks.

Celeriac is a knobbly, globe-shaped root vegetable with a pronounced celery flavour and would certainly never win any beauty contests. It is frequently used as a winter-time ingredient in central European cuisine, and like potato, it combines wonderfully with butter and cream. Serve this tasty and comforting casserole alongside a bold-flavoured partner.

Creamy Celeriac Gratin

serves 4–6 as entrée

2 tablespoons butter

1 teaspoon yellow asafetida powder

1 cup pouring cream

4 tablespoons milk

2 medium celeriac, about 300g (10 ounces) each, peeled and very thinly sliced into rounds

salt

ground white pepper

Preheat the oven to 220°C/425°F.

Melt the butter in a small saucepan over moderate heat. Sprinkle in the yellow asafetida powder and sauté momentarily. Pour in the cream and milk, and heat through for a few minutes, or until warm.

Layer the celeriac in a small baking dish, pouring some of the cream mixture on each layer, along with a sprinkle of salt and white pepper. Pour any remaining sauce over the top layer.

Bake for 15 minutes in the upper centre of the oven, or until golden brown on top, bubbling and approaching tenderness. Carefully cover with foil to avoid over-browning the top layer, and cook for a further 10 minutes or until tender.

Serve hot.

Note: If you are pre-cutting your celeriac, cover with acidulated water to prevent discolouration.

Karhis are smooth yogurt-based dishes served with rice. Either yogurt or buttermilk is whisked with chickpea flour and then simmered into a creamy sauce. Karhi is an excellent source of vegetarian protein — yogurt, a complete protein combines with the chickpea flour — an incomplete protein that becomes complete in conjunction with yogurt. Karhi is delicious, light, easy to digest and good for you — what more could you ask!

Mixed Vegetables in Creamy Karhi Sauce

serves 6

1 ½ cups carrots, peeled and cut into 1.5cm (½-inch) chunks
1 ½ cups green beans, cut 2cm (¾-inch) lengths
1 ½ cups small cauliflower florets
1 ½ cups green peas
2 cups plain yogurt
½ cup chickpea flour *(besan)*
600ml (1 pint) water
1 teaspoon chili powder
½ teaspoon turmeric powder
1 teaspoon coriander powder
2 tablespoons ghee
1 teaspoon brown mustard seeds
1 ½ teaspoons cumin seeds
1 teaspoon yellow asafetida powder
1 ½ teaspoons salt
2 tablespoons chopped fresh coriander leaves

Steam all the vegetables until just tender, drain, cover and set aside.

Whisk together the yogurt with the chickpea flour until smooth and creamy. Add the water, chili powder, turmeric powder and coriander powder, and whisk again.

Heat the ghee in a medium-sized saucepan over moderate heat. When the ghee is fairly hot, sprinkle in the mustard seeds, and fry them until the crackle. Add the cumin, fry until it darkens a few shades, then drop in the yellow asafetida powder and sauté momentarily.

Pour in the yogurt mixture, and, stirring, bring to the boil. Reduce the heat, and simmer for 10 minutes, stirring occasionally.

Fold in the steamed vegetables, the salt and fresh coriander.

Serve hot with rice.

Smoky roasted eggplants mashed and fried with zesty seasonings, then folded with creamy yogurt and fresh herbs — this is baigun bharta, one of Eastern India's most popular dishes. Baigun means eggplant, and the literal meaning of bharta is mashed or puréed. The smoky flavour of the eggplant (reminiscent of Middle Eastern babagannouj) comes from either ash-baking in the coals of a dying fire, oven-baking, or roasting on your stove top.

Purée of Roasted Eggplant
with Seasoned Yogurt

serves 4–6

2 medium-sized eggplants, about 400g (14 ounces) each

2 tablespoons ghee

1 teaspoon cumin seeds

1–2 teaspoons minced hot green chilies

½ teaspoon yellow asafetida powder

1 teaspoon coriander powder

1½ teaspoons salt

2 tablespoons finely-chopped fresh coriander leaves

2 tablespoons finely-chopped mint leaves

1 cup plain yogurt

1 teaspoon *garam masala*

Wash and dry the eggplants, prick them a few times with a fork, rub them all over with a little oil, and lay them directly over burning gas jets on your stovetop.

Cook the eggplants, turning often with tongs, for about 20 minutes, or until the entire surface is blistered and charred, and the flesh is butter-soft. Allow the eggplants to cool briefly, then split the eggplants open and scoop out the smoky soft flesh, discarding the skin.

Coarsely chop the eggplant.

Heat the ghee in a large non-stick frying pan over moderate heat. When fairly hot, drop in the cumin seeds and fry until they darken a few shades, then add the green chilies, frying until aromatic. Sprinkle in the yellow asafetida powder, sauté momentarily then drop in the eggplant, coriander powder and salt. Fry the mixture, stirring often, for about 10 minutes, or until dry and thick.

Transfer the eggplant purée to a bowl and allow it to cool for 2 or 3 minutes. Fold in the fresh herbs, yogurt and *garam masala*.

Serve hot, at room temperature, or chilled, with any flatbread, on whole-grain toast or as a sandwich spread.

Note: Before you commence roasting, place a layer of aluminium foil on the stove top to protect it from drips—it can be a messy business.

There's nothing like the aroma of vegetables roasting in the oven on a cold winter's day. For this recipe, I've done away with baking trays — I've suggested you roast the vegetables directly on the oven racks for maximum speed and even cooking. A fan-forced oven is ideal for this. You will need to place a drip tray on the floor of your oven to catch any juices, and be prepared to give the oven racks a quick scrub as soon as they cool down.

serves 6

¼ cup extra virgin olive oil

1 teaspoon sea salt, or to taste

¼ teaspoon yellow asafetida powder

4 medium pototoes, scrubbed and cut in half

4 medium carrots, scrubbed

4 parsnips, trimmed and scrubbed

¼ medium-sized pumpkin, seeds removed and cut into large chunks

4 small sweet potatoes, scrubbed

6 baby beetroots, scrubbed

¾ cup flat-leaf parsley, finely chopped

1 tablespoon balsamic vinegar, optional

Oven-roasted Vegetables

Whisk together the olive oil, salt and yellow asafetida powder.

Remove one or two racks from the oven, and preheat it to maximum.

Lay out the vegetables directly across the racks, and place them in the oven.

Roast the vegetables for 20 minutes, or until they are tender.

Cool the vegetables slightly, then remove from the oven and toss them in a large bowl with the parsley and the oil mixture. Finally fold through the optional balsamic vinegar.

Serve hot or warm.

This juicy dish features badis, (pronounced like 'buddy'),
Indian sun-dried legume nuggets that add toothsome texture to a variety of dishes.

Vrindavana-style Vegetable Stew

serves 6

2 tablespoons ghee

1 cup yellow *mung badi*, broken
into 1.5 cm (½-inch) pieces

1½ tablespoons grated fresh
ginger

1 teaspoon cumin seeds

4 medium-sized tomatoes, about
300g (11 ounces), peeled and
chopped

½ teaspoon turmeric powder

¼ teaspoon cayenne

3 medium-sized potatoes, about
500g (1 pound), peeled and
diced

4–6 cups water

¼ cup chopped fresh coriander
leaves

1 teaspoon salt

¼ teaspoon black pepper

Heat the ghee over moderate heat in a heavy saucepan. Add the *badi* and pan-fry for about 2 minutes or until lightly browned. Remove with a slotted spoon and set aside.

Fry the ginger and cumin together in the ghee that remains in the pan for 1–2 minutes or until the cumin darkens a few shades.

Stir in the tomatoes, turmeric and cayenne. Cook, stirring occasionally, for about 10 minutes or until the tomatoes are pulpy.

Add the fried *badi*, potatoes, 4 cups water and half the herbs. Bring to the boil, then reduce the heat to medium, partially cover, and cook for about 15–20 minutes or until the potatoes are tender. If necessary, add some extra water.

Fold in the remaining herbs, the salt, pepper, and set aside for 5 minutes before serving.

Serve hot.

To make badi, dried legumes are soaked, drained, wet-ground, seasoned, shaped and sun dried until brittle. They can be stored for years and simply need to be cooked with juicy dishes to re-constitute them. They're full of flavour and power-packed with fat-free protein. The good news for busy cooks is that *badi* (also known as *warian* and *wadi)* can be purchased ready-made at well-stocked Indian grocery stores.
Badi are also great in Mexican chili dishes and pasta sauce.

This is an inspirational short-order dish that works equally well as a side dish or entrée. They are about a quarter of the size of a small cauliflower and are perfect as individual servings. Use baby cauliflower as you would regular cauliflower, but leave the green outer leaves intact — just trim bases.

Baby Cauliflower with Cheese,
Sourdough Breadcrumbs & Toasted Almonds

serves 4

50g (2 ounces) mild, soft blue cheese

100g (4 ounces) *mascarpone* or soft cream cheese

½ teaspoon salt

4 baby cauliflowers, leaves intact and bases trimmed

1 tablespoon olive oil

¼ teaspoon yellow asafetida powder

¾ cup fresh sourdough breadcrumbs

2 tablespoons finely-chopped fresh sage leaves

¼ cup chopped roasted almonds

grindings of black pepper

Whisk the two cheeses with the salt and a little cold water to form a consistency like soft whipped cream.

Steam 4 baby cauliflowers until tender. Drain and keep warm.

Heat the olive oil in a frying pan, sprinkle in the asafetida powder, sauté briefly, add the breadcrumbs and fry, stirring often, for 2–3 minutes or until the breadcrumbs are toasted. Stir in the chopped sage leaves and chopped toasted almonds. Remove from the heat.

Serve: Place cauliflowers on small warmed individual serving dishes, top with spoonfuls of cheese mixture and sprinkle liberally with the combined toasted breadcrumbs, almonds and sage, with a few grindings of black pepper. Serve immediately.

Note: Baby cauliflowers are available throughout the year, but are at their peak in winter.

Mallung is a tasty dry accompaniment of cooked leafy green vegetables that, along with rice, accompanies most Sri Lankan meals. Traditionally, the leaves of many common locally grown plants are used. Choose from any of the leaves listed below, or make up your own combination. Avoid yellow, bruised, spotted or wilted leaves.

Leafy Greens with Coconut (Mallung)

serves 6 as an accompaniment

400g (13 ounces) mixed green leaves—any from the following selection:
spinach, turnip leaves, *gotukolle*, tender passionfruit leaves, parsley, radish leaves, kale, collard greens, mustard greens, fenugreek leaves, cress, sorrel, silverbeet (Swiss chard), beetroot leaves

1 teaspoon minced fresh green chili

¼ teaspoon turmeric

4 tablespoons finely-shredded fresh coconut

½ teaspoon salt

2 teaspoons fresh lemon juice

Carefully wash and drain the leaves in a couple of changes of water.
Steam the leaves in a large heavy-based non-reactive saucepan over low to moderate heat with just the water that is clinging to them, along with the chili and turmeric, for about 6 minutes, or until soft and wilted.
Remove the leaves with a slotted spoon, place on a cutting board, and chop them finely.
Return the spinach to the saucepan with the coconut, salt and lemon. Cook over low heat for a few minutes or until the coconut absorbs the remaining liquid.
Serve hot with rice.

This simple, succulent Italian stew is originally from Naples. In my version I've added fresh basil leaves and olives. It's delicious served as an accompaniment to other dishes, but it's also great served alone with just some fresh crusty bread.

Peppers, Eggplants & Tomatoes
Venetian-style (Peperonata alla Veneta)

serves 4–6

2 tablespoons olive oil

½ teaspoon yellow asafetida powder

4 large sweet yellow or green capsicums (peppers), seeded and sliced

6 large ripe tomatoes, peeled and chopped

one large handful fresh basil leaves, chopped

2 small eggplants, sliced, grilled and chopped, or cubed and pan-fried

¼ cup whole black olives

1 teaspoon salt

½ teaspoon freshly-ground black pepper

1–2 tablespoons extra virgin olive oil, optional

Pour the oil into a heavy saucepan and place over moderate heat. When the oil is hot, sprinkle in the yellow asafetida powder and the sliced capsicums. Fry for 5 minutes, stirring occasionally.

Add the chopped tomatoes and basil leaves, cover with a tight-fitting lid and cook gently for 25 minutes, or until the capsicums are very soft and tender.

Fold in the cooked eggplant, olives, salt and pepper, cook for another 2 minutes, then remove from the heat.

Serve hot or cold drizzled with the optional extra virgin olive oil.

Tender chickpeas and buttery spinach folded through aromatic tomato sauce appear on many a Middle Eastern dinner table. This sensational Saudi version is flavoured with a popular spice blend called baharat, a generic blend of herbs and spices that varies according to the taste of the spice merchant. My favourite combination is pepper, cumin, coriander, cinnamon, cloves, cardamom, paprika and nutmeg. Baharat, which is available at Middle Eastern grocers, is added towards the end of the cooking, much like garam masala is used in Indian cuisine.

Chickpeas with Spinach (Hoummos bi Sabanik)

serves 4

3 tablespoons ghee or olive oil
1 teaspoon yellow asafetida powder
1 cup tomato purée
375g (13 ounces) cooked chickpeas, about 3 cups
450g (1 pound) spinach, leaves, steamed, blanched and chopped
1 teaspoon salt
½ teaspoon freshly-cracked black pepper
1 teaspoon brown sugar
1 teaspoon *baharat*
extra 2 tablespoons ghee or olive oil for garnish
1 tablespoon fresh lemon juice for garnish
2 or 3 tablespoons freshly-chopped parsley for garnish

Heat the ghee or oil in a medium saucepan over moderate heat. Sprinkle in the yellow asafetida powder and sauté momentarily.

Pour in the tomato purée, and cook, stirring occasionally, for about 2–3 minutes or until slightly reduced.

Fold the cooked chickpeas into the tomato purée, along with the blanched spinach, the salt, pepper, sugar and *baharat*.

Reduce the heat and cook for an extra 2–3 minutes.

Serve hot, garnished with drizzles of the remaining ghee or olive oil, lemon juice and a sprinkle of fresh parsley, accompanied by thirsty flatbreads to mop up the fragrant juices.

Vegetarian Barbeque

Salsa verde simply means green sauce — there are hundreds of versions. This one, smothered over slabs of barbecued haloumi cheese and grilled juicy asparagus, is made from the 'big three': parsley, mint and basil. It's perked up with a smattering of tasty capers.

Barbecued Haloumi and Char-grilled Asparagus
with Salsa Verde

serves 4 as an entrée

16 spears of asparagus, about 2
  bunches, trimmed

4 bamboo skewers, soaked in hot
  water for 15 minutes

400g (14 ounces) *haloumi* cheese,
  thickly sliced

olive oil

Salsa Verde

1 cup flat-leaf parsley, finely
  chopped

½ cup mint leaves, finely chopped

½ cup basil leaves, finely chopped

2 tablespoons capers, rinsed,
  drained and chopped

¼ teaspoon yellow asafetida
  powder

$^2/_3$ cup olive oil

¼ cup lemon juice

salt and pepper to taste

Combine all the *salsa verde* ingredients in a bowl.

Thread 4 asparagus spears onto each skewer.

Brush the asparagus and *haloumi* generously with olive oil.

Barbecue the asparagus for 2 minutes each side or until just tender.

Barbecue the *haloumi* on a hot plate for 2 minutes each side, or until golden.

Serve: Slide the asparagus off their skewers, place a large spoonful of *salsa verde* onto 4 plates and top with asparagus and *haloumi*. Pass the remaining *salsa* separately.

Vegie Burgers 'With the Lot'

I was searching far and wide for a quick vegie burger recipe, and found a great one, quite by chance, on an Internet cooking seminar for kids. Here it is, slightly improved, courtesy of Jayasri Devi of Crescent City, California.

Mix together the oatmeal, herbs and asafetida in a bowl and pour on the boiling water. Mix well and set aside for 5 minutes.

Fold in all the other ingredients thoroughly, and knead the mixture until very well combined.

Scoop up quantities of mix using a ½-cup measuring cup, pack and press the ½ cup full, then shake or tap the cup to remove the thick burger patty. Gently press and form it into a larger, smooth burger patty, and proceed on with the rest of the mixture. Heat oil in a frying pan.

Pan fry the burgers, a batch at a time, until dark golden brown on each side. Remove and drain on paper towels.

Serve on buns with all your favourite 'fixins'.

makes 16 burgers

2 cups fine oatmeal

2 teaspoons Italian mixed herbs

1 teaspoon yellow asafetida powder

1½ cups boiling water

½ cup peanut butter

½ cup cooked chickpeas, minced fine

2 cups dry breadcrumbs

5 tablespoons soy sauce

1½ teaspoon salt

½ cup very finely chopped celery

2 tablespoons tomato paste

¼ cup finely-chopped parsley

oil for pan-frying

burger buns and all the trimmings of your choice

Trio of Roasted, Grilled or Barbecued Vegetables

Potatoes, pumpkin and sweet potatoes are all suitable for oven roasting, grilling or barbecuing over hot coals, either directly or wrapped in foil. Whichever way you choose, the accompanying pesto, salsa and chutney transform these earthy vegetables into something very special.

White Sweet Potato with Fresh Corn Chutney

The brilliant corn chutney has become one of my favourites. It marries perfectly with sweet potato, its South American partner from ages past. Best consumed the day it's made.

- 2 cups cooked fresh corn kernels, or 2 cups frozen corn kernels, thawed
- 1½ cups firmly packed coriander leaves, coarsely chopped
- ¼ cup packed fresh mint
- 1 small hot green chili, coarsely chopped
- 2 tablespoons coarsely-chopped fresh ginger
- 1 teaspoon sugar
- 1 teaspoon salt
- ½ teaspoon freshly-ground black pepper
- juice of 1 large lime
- little water if needed
- 1 kilo (2 pounds) scrubbed unpeeled white sweet potatoes, roasted, grilled or barbecued

Process all the chutney ingredients in a food processor, pulsing on and off until the mixture is slightly chunky and loose textured. Add a little water if the mixture is too firm. **Serve** immediately with the sweet potato, or cover and refrigerate. Serves 4.

Pumpkin with Mango Salsa

A brilliantly zesty accompaniment featuring sweet, sour, hot and aromatic flavours.

- 1 large ripe mango cut into small cubes
- ½ cup diced, unpeeled cucumber
- ¼ teaspoon yellow asafetida powder
- 2 tablespoons finely-chopped fresh mint leaves
- 1 teaspoon finely-shredded fresh red chilies
- 2 tablespoons fresh lime juice
- 1 teaspoon salt
- 1 teaspoon black pepper
- 1 kilo (2 pounds) pumpkin pieces, trimmed and cut into suitable chunks, roasted, grilled or barbecued

Combine all the *salsa* ingredients and allow flavours to combine for a few minutes.
Serve with the roasted pumpkins.
Serves 4.

Idaho Potatoes with Parsley Pesto

Parley pesto is nutty, green and luscious—a perfect foil for creamy hot potato.

- 1 kilo (2 pounds) Idaho baking potatoes, roasted, grilled or barbecued
- 1 cup flat-leaf parsley
- ½ teaspoon yellow asafetida powder
- ¼ teaspoon freshly-grated nutmeg
- ¼ cup toasted almonds
- 1 tablespoon lemon juice
- ½ teaspoon salt
- 2 tablespoons olive oil

Combine all the *pesto* ingredients except the oil in a food processor and process until smooth. With the motor running, slowly drizzle in the oil. When well amalgamated, remove and serve. Add a few drops of water if the mixture is too thick. **Serve** with the roasted potatoes. **Serves 4.**

Char-grilled Turkish Bread
with Greek-style Salad

A luscious and full-bodied Greek salad with grilled Turkish bread — gastronomically correct!

serves 6

250g (½ pound) cherry tomatoes, halved

2 Lebanese cucumbers cut into 2cm (¾-inch) pieces

200g (7 ounces) marinated *feta*

4 tablespoons small, drained capers

100g (3 ounces) marinated drained artichokes, quartered

handful basil leaves, torn

1 tablespoon chopped mint

2 tablespoons extra virgin olive oil

2 tablespoons lemon juice

1 loaf Turkish bread *(pide)* halved lengthwise and cut into large triangles

more olive oil for brushing

salt and pepper to taste

Combine the tomato, cucumber, *feta*, capers, artichokes and herbs in a large bowl.

Whisk together the extra virgin olive oil and lemon juice until well combined, pour over the salad and mix gently.

Brush the Turkish bread with a little olive oil and char-grill over high heat until golden on both sides.

Serve: Place a bread triangle on each of the 6 serving plates, top with salad and serve with another triangle of bread on the side. Season to taste. Pass around the remaining bread separately.

Spanish-style Charcoal-grilled Vegetables (Escalivada)

Eggplants and capsicums (peppers) roasted over hot coals and ashes of an open fire or barbecue become infused with rich nutty flavours and a delicious smoky aroma.

serves 6

4 small Japanese eggplants

3 large red capsicums (peppers)

3 large green capsicums (peppers)

6 small to medium sun-ripened tomatoes

½ cup virgin olive oil

1 teaspoon salt

1 teaspoon freshly-ground black pepper

Place the whole eggplants and capsicums directly on a barbecue grid or into a gently glowing wood or charcoal outdoors fire.

Roast the vegetables, turning frequently with tongs, until their skins are very dark and the vegetables are soft to the touch.

Cut a cross in the top of each tomato, and either cook them directly on the barbecue or fry them in a pan with a little olive oil. Peel them.

Remove the eggplants and peppers and peel off their charred skin. Thinly slice the eggplant, and tear the peppers into strips.

Serve: Arrange on warmed serving plates, placing the tomatoes in the centre. Whisk the oil, salt and pepper together, and pour on liberally.

Escalivada

Escalivada is one of the signature dishes of Spain's Catalan cuisine. The word literally means 'grilling over charcoal'. A simple seasoning of a little salt and generous splashes of Spanish olive oil transform these homely vegetables into a feast. The versatile *Escalivada* can be served as a hot vegetable accompaniment to other dishes, as *tapas* or hors d'oeuvre, or as an appetizer in the manner of the Italian marinated vegetable *antipasto*. It can also be presented as a cold salad, or mashed to a purée and spread on chunks of toasted bread. *Escalivada* can be made in the oven, as is done even in some Catalonian restaurants, but with a noticeable loss of the unique smoky flavour.

Despite the fact that okra, the seed-pod of the plant Abelmoschus esculentusis is enjoyed the world over, for many cooks okra is still an unknown vegetable. If this is your first experience of okra, I think you'll enjoy this recipe.

Barbecued Baby Okra with Herbed Butter

makes 16 skewers

32 firm, fresh baby okra pods
sage butter (recipe follows)
thyme butter (recipe follows)

Soak 16 short skewers in hot water for 15 minutes.

Blanch the okra pods in a large saucepan of boiling water. Remove and drain them.

Thread 2 okra pods lengthwise on each skewer.

Grill the okra over hot coals for 6–7 minutes or until slightly browned, brushing two or three times with the herb butter of your choice.

Serve hot with a drizzle more of herb butter.

Thyme Butter

50g (2 ounces) butter, about ı
    cup
2 sprigs fresh thyme, or
    ½ teaspoon dried thyme
½ teaspoon ground cumin

Melt the butter and combine with the thyme and cumin.

Sage Butter

50g (2 ounces) butter, about
    ¼ cup
3 or 4 sprigs sage, or 1 teaspoon
    crumbled dried sage
¼ teaspoon freshly-grated nutmeg

Melt the butter and combine with the sage and nutmeg.

The size of okra pods determines which recipes they are best used in. Large pods generally possess a fine flavour, but they usually have fibrous, tough spines running lengthwise along the sides from cap to tail. Medium pods are large enough to endure stuffing, while baby pods are perfect for slicing or leaving whole, as in the case of this delicious barbecued baby okra. Select firm, fresh baby pods no longer than 5-8 cm (2-3 inches).

Caponata is the famous antipasto salad from Italy consisting of fried eggplants, tomatoes, capers and olives. I've adapted the recipe to produce a juicier version that lends itself well to grilled polenta.

Barbecued Polenta with Rocket Leaves, Caponata Sauce & Parmesan

serves 6

1.5 litres/quarts water
1 teaspoon salt
1 ½ cups polenta
olive oil
caponata sauce (recipe follows)
rocket leaves for serving
shavings of Parmesan

Bring the water to a boil, add the salt, whisk in the polenta, and stir constantly over medium heat for 2–3 minutes. Reduce the heat to low, and cook, stirring occasionally for 15 minutes or until very thick.

Spoon the polenta into an oiled 23cm (9-inch) square cake tin, smooth the surface and refrigerate until firm.

Cut the polenta into 12 triangles. Brush generously with olive oil, and barbecue or char-grill for 5–6 minutes each side until browned.

Serve: Place the polenta on serving plates, and top with rocket, *caponata* and shavings of Parmesan cheese.

Note: For a quicker polenta cooking time, try using instant polenta, which you'll find at good delicatessens. Cook according to instructions on the packet.

Caponata Sauce

¼ cup virgin olive oil
½ teaspoon yellow asafetida powder
1 large eggplant cut into 1.25cm
　　(½-inch) cubes
1 large red capsicum (pepper) cut into
　　1.25cm (½-inch) cubes
2 cups tomato purée
1 teaspoon salt
2 tablespoons chopped fresh basil leaves
¼ cup pitted black olives, chopped
1 tablespoon sugar
¼ teaspoon freshly-ground black pepper
2 tablespoons brine-packed capers,
　　rinsed and drained

Heat the olive oil in a saucepan over moderate heat. When hot, sprinkle in the yellow asafetida powder and the eggplant pieces.

Fry the eggplant for 2–3 minutes, then add the capsicum and fry for another 10–15 minutes, or until the eggplants are tender.

Pour in the tomato purée, add the salt and basil, increase the heat and cook for another 5 minutes, or until the sauce is a little reduced. Fold in the olives, sugar, black pepper and capers.

Serve with the grilled polenta.

Spicy Grilled Corn on the Cob

Everyone has a different method of grilling corn. Here are two tried and tested methods. I've also included four different ways to season your corn. Happy shucking!

serves 4
(allowing 2 corn cobs per person)

Two Ways of Grilling Corn

Method One:

Pull back the husks, remove the silks, tie the husks back on, and soak the ears in cold water for 20 minutes. **Grill** the corn over hot coals, turning occasionally, for 15–20 minutes. This method steams the corn inside the husk, and the charred husk perfumes the corn as well.

Method Two:

Shuck the corn completely and oil it lightly.
Roast it in a covered barbecue for 10–15 minutes, turning occasionally.

Corn with Herbed Butter

½ cup unsalted butter, softened
2 teaspoons finely-chopped fresh dill
2 teaspoons freshly-chopped fresh parsley
sea salt, freshly ground
butter to taste
8 corn cobs, grilled

Mix the butter with the herbs.
Serve: Spread liberally on the grilled corn.

Corn with Jalapeño and Cumin Butter

½ cup softened unsalted butter
2 teaspoons finely-chopped fresh or pickled *jalapeño* chilies
1 teaspoon cumin seeds, toasted and ground
1 tablespoon choppe   d fresh coriander
8 corn cobs, grilled

Mix all the ingredients.
Serve: Rub on your hot grilled corn.

> **If you prefer boiled corn, here's a few hints:**
> If your corn is young and fresh, remove the husks and boil it for a maximum of 2 minutes in rapidly boiling unsalted water (salted water makes the kernels tough). Don't crowd the ears —cook no more than 6 at a time in 4 litres (one gallon) of water. Serve the corn as soon as it's cooked. The guests should wait for the corn, not vice-versa.
> If your corn is a little older or has been refrigerated, boil it for 5 minutes, and add 2 tablespoons sugar in the water to improve the flavour.

Mediterranean-style Corn on the Cob

8 corn cobs, grilled

extra-virgin olive oil, to taste

sea salt and freshly-ground black pepper to taste

hot red pepper flakes (optional)

Drizzle the grilled corn with the oil.

Serve: Sprinkled with the salt, pepper and optional hot red pepper flakes.

Mexican-style Corn on the Cob

¼ cup salt

ground red chili, to taste

2 limes, cut in half

8 corn cobs, grilled

Mix the salt and chili in a small bowl.

Serve: Dip the cut side of the lime into the salt-chili mixture and rub it down the length of the ear of corn. Squeeze on more lime juice to taste.

Most people associate maple syrup with pancakes, waffles, ice-cream or puddings. Here it plays a part in a savoury context, as a main player in a marinade for crusty pan-fried panir steaks.

Panir Steaks with Maple Syrup Marinade,
Sweet Potato Mash & Rocket Salad

serves 6

2 tablespoons olive oil

½ teaspoon yellow asafetida powder

6 *panir* steaks (recipe follows)

sweet potato mash to serve (recipe follows)

rocket salad to serve (recipe follows)

Marinade

3 tablespoons maple syrup

¼ teaspoon cayenne pepper

1 tablespoon tomato paste

1 tablespoon soy sauce

1 tablespoon dijon or seed mustard

2 tablespoons lemon juice

3 tablespoons water

Whisk together all the marinade ingredients in a bowl.

Heat the olive oil in a ridged grill pan placed over fairly high heat. Sprinkle in the yellow asafetida powder and sauté momentarily.

Fry the *panir* steaks in the flavoured oil on both sides until crusty, then pour over the marinade. Cook the *panir* steaks, turning until the liquid is slightly reduced, then remove from the heat.

Serve the *panir* steaks on sweet potato mash with any pan juices poured over, accompanied by the rocket salad.

Rocket Salad

1 tablespoon olive oil

1 tablespoon lemon juice

salt and pepper to taste

100g (4 ounces) rocket leaves

Whisk together the olive oil, lemon juice, salt and pepper.

Pour over the rocket leaves.

Sweet Potato Mash

1 kg (2 pounds) orange or white sweet-potato, sliced thick

2 tablespoons melted butter, or more to taste

1 teaspoon salt

½ teaspoon freshly- ground black pepper

Boil the sweet potato in lightly salted water until tender. Drain.

Mash thoroughly and mix in the butter, salt and black pepper.

Panir Steaks

5 litres/quarts fresh milk

3–4 cups yogurt or 6–8 tablespoons lemon juice

Heat the milk to boiling point in a heavy-based saucepan.

Stir in ¾ of the yogurt or lemon juice. The milk should separate into chunky curds, leaving a greenish liquid residue called whey. If not completely separated, add a little more yogurt or lemon juice. Drape a double thickness of cheesecloth over a colander placed in the sink.

Scoop out the curds with a slotted spoon and place them in the cheese-cloth. Pour the whey, along with remaining curds in the saucepan, into the cheesecloth. Gather the ends of the cloth together and hold the bag of curd cheese under cold running water for 30 seconds. Twist the bag tightly to squeeze out extra whey, return it to the colander.

Press under a heavy weight for 10–15 minutes. Carefully remove the curd cheese from the cloth. Your *panir* is ready. Slice into 6 steaks.

Grilled Ciabatta
with Syrian Roast Pepper & Walnut Paste

Here I'm serving grilled ciabatta (the oval Italian bread named after a slipper)
with the exotic muhammara paste, along with bite-sized blanched vegetables (crudites)
of your choice. Great for a picnic or an alfresco lunch.

makes 1½ cups paste

2 large red capsicums (peppers)

1 small hot red chili, seeded and
   chopped

1 slice wholemeal bread, crusts
   removed

1 cup shelled walnuts

½ teaspoon yellow asafetida powder

1½ tablespoons pomegranate
   molasses

juice of ½ lemon

½ teaspoon sugar

½ teaspoon salt

3 tablespoons extra virgin olive oil

1 tablespoon flat-leaf parsley

toasted *ciabatta* bread, to serve

vegetable *crudites*, to serve

Roast the capsicums under a grill for 15 minutes, or until the skin is blistered and blackened. Place in a plastic bag, seal and set aside for 5 minutes before peeling. Alternatively, grill the capsicums in the coals of a barbecue.

Combine all the ingredients except the parsley *ciabatta* and *crudites* in a food processor and blend to a thick creamy paste.

Serve sprinkled with the parsley, and accompanied with chunks of toasted *ciabatta* and the vegetable *crudites*.

Muhammara Paste
There are many versions of the delicious paste known as *muhammara* all over the Middle East; this one is from Syria. The sourness of *muhammara* comes from pomegranate concentrate, sometimes called pomegranate molasses—thick, sour and fruity syrup available in bottles or jars from Middle Eastern grocers. The sweet and sour, nutty paste couples well with bread or lightly blanched vegetables.

Pasta and Grains

Potato Gnocchi in Gorgonzola Sauce

This rich, irresistible dish is based on a classic sauce prepared up and down the length of Italy.
Enjoy it when calories are not a consideration. I have suggested a mild, sweet Gorgonzola cheese,
dolce latte. A mild Danish Blue yields equally stunning results. The sauce works equally well with pasta.

serves 4

500g (1 pound) ready-to-cook potato *gnocchi*
2 tablespoons butter
½ teaspoon yellow asafetida powder
200ml (1/3 pint) light pouring cream
200g (7 ounces) mild sweet Gorgonzola cheese
½ teaspoon salt
¼ teaspoon black pepper
few gratings nutmeg

Boil the *gnocchi* as per instructions on the packet.
Melt the butter in a large saucepan over low to medium heat, sprinkle in the yellow asafetida powder, and sauté momentarily. Pour in a little cream, crumble in the cheese, and stir through until the cheese has melted completely and the ingredients have been combined.
Stir in the rest of the cream, the salt, pepper, gratings of nutmeg. Without allowing the sauce to boil, heat for another 5 minutes or until the sauce has assumed the quality of thick cream. Fold in the cooked, drained *gnocchi*.
Serve immediately.

Pasta Shells Stuffed with
Spinach, Herbs & White Cheese

Giant, conch-shaped pasta, conchiglie gigante, is a quick alternative to cannelloni. In this recipe, their cavities are filled with creamy ricotta folded with spinach, fresh basil and Parmesan cheese. The pasta shells are lightly drizzled with a homemade tomato sauce, and topped with shredded rocket leaves and shaved Parmesan.

serves 6

350g (12 ounces) giant conch pasta, cooked until
  al dente, drained

½ bunch rocket, finely shredded, for garnish

shaved Parmesan, for garnish

Sauce

1 tablespoon olive oil

½ teaspoon yellow asafetida powder

½ dried basil leaves

½ teaspoon dried oregano leaves

2 cups tomato purée

1 teaspoon salt

1 teaspoon sugar

Filling

800g (1¾ pounds) ricotta cheese, drained of whey

1½ tablespoons olive oil

3 tablespoons sour cream

¼ teaspoon nutmeg

1½ teaspoons salt

¾ teaspoon pepper

¾ cup grated Parmesan cheese

200g (7 ounces) spinach, weighed without stems,
  blanched, squeezed dry, and chopped

50g (2 ounces) fresh basil leaves, about 1 packed
  cup

Combine all the filling ingredients in a large bowl and mix well.

Cook the sauce: Heat the olive oil in a medium pan over moderate heat, sprinkle in the yellow asafetida powder and dried herbs and sauté momentarily. Pour in the tomato purée, add the salt and sugar and cook for about 5 minutes, or until slightly reduced.

Spoon sufficient filling into each shell, ensuring the pasta is not over-stuffed. Arrange the pasta shells on a large baking tray and drizzle with the hot sauce.

Warm the pasta through in a moderate oven for 5 minutes.

Serve: Arrange a few pasta shells on warmed plates and top with shredded rocket and shaved Parmesan.

Mung Beans, Rice & Vegetables (Khichari)

Khichari (pronounced 'kitch-eri') is such an important dish for vegetarians that I have included a different recipe for it in each of my cookbooks. The flavoursome, juicy stew of mung beans, rice and vegetables is both nutritious and sustaining. It can be served any time a one-pot meal is required. You can practically live on khichari, and in fact some people do. I eat it accompanied by a little yogurt, some whole-wheat toast, lemon or lime wedges and topped with a drizzle of melted ghee. Bliss!

serves 4–6

½ cup split mung beans, washed and drained

6 cups water

1 bay leaf

1.5cm (½-inch) chunk ginger, chopped fine

1 small green chili, seeded and chopped

½ teaspoon turmeric

2 teaspoons coriander powder

1 cup Thai rice, or other long-grain rice of your choice

1 packed cup each broccoli, potato cubes and quartered Brussels sprouts, or vegetables of your choice

2 ripe tomatoes, chopped

1½ teaspoons salt

2 tablespoons ghee

2 teaspoons cumin seeds

small handful curry leaves

½ teaspoon yellow asafetida powder

½ cup chopped fresh coriander leaves

wedges of lemon, some chilled yogurt, and extra ghee for serving

Bring to a boil the mung beans, water, bay leaf, ginger, chili, turmeric and coriander in a saucepan, then reduce to a simmer, and cook, partially covered, for about 15 minutes or until the beans start to break up.

Add the rice, vegetables, tomatoes and salt, increase the heat, and stirring, bring to a boil, then return to a simmer, covered. Stirring occasionally, cook for another 10–15 minutes, or until the rice is soft.

Season: Heat the ghee in a small saucepan over moderate heat. Sprinkle in the cumin seeds, fry until a few shades darker, and add the curry leaves—careful, they crackle. Sprinkle in the yellow asafetida powder, swirl the pan and empty the fried seasonings into the *khichari*. Stir the seasonings through, then return to a simmer and cook for another 5 minutes or so, or until the rice is fully swollen and soft. If you desire a moist *khichari*, add a little boiling water now.

Serve: Fold in the fresh coriander, and serve the *khichari* piping hot with a drizzle of warm ghee, and the accompaniments suggested above.

Chickpea Cutlets with
New Mexico Chili & Tomato Salsa

Chickpeas are not only packed full of valuable nutrients, they're also versatile. These attractive patties come with a tasty oven-caramelised salsa. Add a salad and you have a substantial meal. If you commence the salsa first, it should be ready to serve with the cutlets.

makes 24 cutlets

4 cups cooked chickpeas, rinsed and drained

½ cup coriander leaves

½ cup fresh mint leaves

1 tablespoon chopped fresh ginger

3 green chilies, seeded and chopped

2 teaspoons ground cumin

2½ teaspoons salt

1 teaspoon freshly-cracked black pepper

²/₃ cup fresh or frozen corn kernels

2 cups fresh breadcrumbs

5 small red capsicums (peppers), roasted, peeled, seeded and diced small

oil for pan-frying

Combine the chickpeas, coriander, mint, ginger, chilies, cumin, salt and pepper in a food processor. **Pulse** until coarsely chopped. Add the corn and pulse a little more until the corn is slightly broken. Transfer the mixture to a bowl.

Fold in the breadcrumbs and diced capsicums. Mix to fully incorporate the breadcrumbs. The mixture should be fairly stiff. Add more breadcrumbs if necessary.

Form the mixture into 24 patties with moistened palms. Pour sufficient oil in a frying pan for pan-frying and place over moderately high heat.

Pan-fry the patties in the hot oil in batches, cooking them 3–4 minutes on each side, or until well browned. Drain on paper towels.

Serve warm with the chili and tomato *salsa*.

New Mexico Chili and Tomato Salsa

A full-bodied, hot and smoky *salsa* redolent with the earthy flavour and distinct mild heat of New Mexico chilies (sometimes referred to as Colorado or California chilies).

3 large dried New Mexico chilies

6 ripe tomatoes, blanched, peeled, seeded and chopped

1 tablespoon olive oil

1 tablespoon brown sugar

salt

Soak the chilies in hot water for 20 minutes, or until soft. Drain them, remove the stems, and then finely chop the chilies. Preheat the oven to 220°C/425°F.

Combine all the ingredients in an ovenproof pan.

Bake for about 20 minutes or until the tomatoes start to caramelise and turn brown.

Serve at room temperature with the chickpea cutlets. Makes about 1½ cups.

Millet is a light, versatile and inviting grain with a mild, nutty taste, distinctive without being unusual. To bring out the flavour in millet, the tiny yellow grains are toasted in butter or oil before cooking in stock or water. Millet is a thirsty grain, so serve this pilaff alongside a juicy vegetable dish or soup.

Millet Pilaff with Corn, Peppers and Pine Nuts

serves 6

2 ½ cups water or vegetable stock
½ cup frozen corn kernels
1 cup tomatoes, diced fine
1 teaspoon salt
¼ teaspoon black pepper
2 tablespoons butter, olive oil, or a combination
1 teaspoon yellow asafetida powder
2 teaspoons julienned fresh ginger root
2 small green chilies, seeded and chopped
¾ cup diced red capsicum (pepper)
1 ¼ cups hulled millet
¼ cup toasted pine nuts

Combine the stock, corn, tomato, salt and pepper in a small saucepan. Bring to a boil and simmer, fully covered, over low heat.

Heat the oil or butter in a saucepan over moderate heat. Add the yellow asafetida powder, the ginger, chili, green capsicum and the millet.

Sauté the millet for 3–4 minutes, or until it darkens a few shades.

Pour the simmering stock into the toasted grains, bring to the boil, reduce the heat to low, cover, and cook for about 20 minutes, or until the liquid has been absorbed and the grains are soft. Set aside for 5 minutes to firm up.

Serve hot with a sprinkle of toasted pine nuts.

I remember growing up with macaroni cheese. Although it's a little out of fashion in today's multi-cuisine society, it still remains one of my favourites.

Traditional Macaroni Cheese

serves 4

300g (10 ounces) tubular pasta
90g (3 ounces) butter
3 tablespoons flour
2 cups milk
1 cup cream
100g (3 ounces) tasty cheese, grated
½ teaspoon freshly-ground black pepper
good pinch freshly-grated nutmeg
2 tablespoons grated Parmesan cheese

Preheat the oven to 180°C/350°F.

Cook the pasta according to the directions on the packet. Drain and transfer to a lightly oiled casserole dish.

Melt the butter in a medium-sized saucepan. Sprinkle in the flour and cook for 2 minutes, stirring continuously. Remove from the heat and gradually whisk in the milk and cream. Return to the heat and bring to the boil, stirring until the mixture thickens. Add the cheese, pepper and nutmeg, and mix well.

Pour the sauce over the pasta and mix thoroughly until evenly coated. Sprinkle the Parmesan cheese over the top.

Bake in the oven for 10 minutes, or until the top is golden brown.

Serve hot.

In Thailand, the home of this dish, the ingredients vary according to what's in season and what's on hand, and is very much open to improvisation. Knowing this, I made up a vegetarian version. Mee krob is always a big favourite at parties and special event dinners because of the way it looks — colourful, sweet and sour vegetables mounted on noodles that puff up dramatically when deep fried.

Crispy Fried Noodles with Sweet & Sour Sauce (Mee Krob)

serves 4

peanut oil for deep frying

125g (4 ounces) rice vermicelli

1 tablespoon minced fresh ginger

1 hot red chili, minced

½ teaspoon yellow asafetida powder

1 large carrot cut into long matchsticks

120g (4 ounces) snake beans, cut into
2cm (1-inch) lengths

1 large zucchini cut into 2cm
(1-inch) batons

2 small capsicums (peppers) cut into 1cm
(½-inch) cubes

150g (5 ounces) fried bean curd puffs,
cut into 1cm (½-inch) cubes

100g (3 ounces) bean sprouts

Sauce

2 tablespoons palm sugar, grated fine

½ teaspoon freshly-cracked black pepper

¼ cup fresh lime juice

1 teaspoon *sambal oelek*

1 tablespoon sweet chili sauce

4 tablespoons vegetarian oyster sauce

Garnish

2 fresh red chilies, sliced

½ cup coriander leaves

a few bean shoots

Whisk together all the sauce ingredients in a small bowl until the sugar dissolves. Set aside.

Heat oil in a wok over full heat until almost smoking. Cut the rice vermicelli into manageable lengths with scissors.

Deep-fry a handful of noodles at a time. The noodles will immediately puff up—remove them immediately, and place in a colander. Pour off most of the oil, leaving 1 tablespoon. Return the wok to the heat.

Fry the ginger and chilies for 1–2 minutes, or until aromatic. Sprinkle in the yellow asafetida powder followed by the carrots and a couple of tablespoons of water. Cover the wok and steam the carrots for 2 minutes. Drop in the beans and zucchini, and replace the lid. Cook for another 2 minutes. Lift the lid, throw in the capsicums and tofu. Fry uncovered, stirring occasionally, for 1 minute. Add the sprouts.

Stir in the sauce. Cook for 30 seconds more then remove from the heat.

Serve: Place most of the fried noodles on a large serving platter. Pour on the sauce, and scatter with the reserved chili, coriander leaves and bean sprouts. Top with the rest of the crisp noodles, bring to the table and serve. Even better—fry the noodles in front of the guests.

Pasta Spirals with Spinach & Walnut Pesto

Pesto was so called because it was traditionally pounded in a mortar and pestle. You can still do it, of course, although a food processor seems appropriate these fast-moving days. Walnuts make a delicious pesto — known as salsa di noci — and mixed with raw puréed spinach marry wonderfully with a pasta such as spirali.

serves 4

125g (4 ounces) walnut pieces, about 1ı cups

300g (10 ounces) young tender spinach leaves, washed and dried

¼ cup olive oil

½ cup Parmesan cheese

1 teaspoon salt

½ teaspoon freshly-cracked black pepper

400g (14 ounces) pasta spirals

2 tablespoons chopped walnuts, reserved

Toast the walnuts on a baking tray in a hot oven (200°C/400°F) for 7–10 minutes, or until aromatic and lightly toasted, then remove and cool.

Process the cooled walnuts and spinach in a food processor until finely chopped and combined. With the motor running, gradually add the olive oil in a thin stream and process until the mixture is fully blended. Add the Parmesan, salt and pepper and process for one more minute. Remove the *pesto*.

Boil the pasta in plenty of salted water according to the directions on the packet, then drain it.

Stir the spinach and walnut *pesto* through the hot-cooked spiral pasta.

Serve: Spoon into serving bowls and sprinkle with the reserved chopped walnuts.

Note: Spinach and walnut *pesto* combines beautifully with tender steamed baby potatoes or roasted peeled pumpkin pieces.

If you haven't got the time to prepare your own ravioli pastry, frozen eggless wonton wrappers are an ideal alternative. They come in round or square varieties, although I prefer the large square type. Stuffed with sage-flavoured pumpkin and drizzled with brown butter, they make a delightful entree for six or a substantial course in a meal for four.

Pumpkin Ravioli with Baby Spinach & Brown Butter

4 main serves or 6 entrées

500g (1 pound) butternut pumpkin, peeled and cut into large chunks

1 or 2 tablespoons chopped fresh sage leaves

¼ teaspoon yellow asafetida powder

1 teaspoon salt

½ teaspoon freshly-cracked black pepper

1–2 tablespoons dried breadcrumbs

40 square eggless wonton wrappers

100g (3 ounces) unsalted butter

100g (3 ounces) baby spinach to serve

100g (3 ounces) Parmesan, finely grated

Steam the pumpkin over boiling water until tender.

Mash and combine with the sage, asafetida, salt, pepper and sufficient breadcrumbs to soak up any excess moisture. Set aside to cool.

Place 6 wonton wrappers on a floured bench and place one heaped tablespoon of pumpkin mixture in the centre of each. Rub the edges of the pastry with some water, top with another wrapper and press the edges together firmly, pressing with the tines of a fork if preferred. Repeat with the remaining wrappers and pumpkin filling.

Cook each batch of ravioli in simmering salted water for 2 minutes. Remove with a slotted spoon and drain.

Serve: Melt the butter in a saucepan and heat until foaming and nut-brown in colour. Place baby spinach leaves on warmed serving plates, top with 4 or 5 ravioli, sprinkle with Parmesan and drizzle with the browned butter.

Mock Crab Cakes with
Thai Peanut & Cucumber Relish

Soaked and ground split yellow mung beans with shredded cabbage are the basis of these tasty fried savouries.

makes about 40

1½ cups split yellow mung beans, soaked
    overnight and drained

2cm (¾-inch) chunk peeled fresh ginger

1 or 2 teaspoon, chopped fresh lemongrass

2 teaspoons salt

1½ tablespoons coriander powder

½ teaspoon dried red chili flakes

1 teaspoon yellow asafetida powder

¼ cup fresh parsley

¼ cup fresh coriander

4 cups freshly shredded cabbage

½ teaspoon baking powder

oil for deep frying

Process the mung beans and ginger together in a food processor until coarsely chopped. Add the lemongrass, salt, coriander powder, red chili flakes, asafetida, parsley and coriander and process until the herbs are minced. Transfer to a bowl.

Fold in the cabbage and baking powder, and mix well. Divide the mixture into about 40 cakes.

Heat oil for deep-frying in a wok or deep pan. When the oil reaches about 180°C/350°F, lower in a batch of cakes.

Deep fry them until golden brown on both sides, remove and drain.

Serve warm with the peanut and cucumber relish.

Thai Peanut & Cucumber Relish

½ cup white vinegar or lemon juice

4 tablespoons palm sugar, finely shredded

1 teaspoon salt

½ cup water

4 tablespoons vegetarian oyster sauce

1 red chili, chopped fine

½ medium cucumber, peeled and thinly
    sliced

1 tablespoon finely-chopped fresh
    coriander leaves

3 tablespoons chopped roasted peanuts

Whisk together the vinegar or lemon juice with the sugar, salt and water until the sugar dissolves. Add the vegetarian oyster sauce and the chopped chili.

Serve: Layer the cucumber slices in a small bowl, sprinkle with coriander leaves, pour over the sweet-sour sauce and top with the peanuts. Serve with the fried mock crab cakes.

Note: For a low-fat version, pan-fry the mock crab cakes on a lightly oiled griddle.

Bocconcini—little balls of snowy white fresh mozzarella cheese that come floating in whey—
is one of my favourite cheeses. Farfalle is pasta in the shape of a butterfly, or bow tie, depending
on how you look at it. The simply seasoned, unassertive tomato sauce brings everything together
wonderfully and allows the cheese to melt to an unsurpassed succulence.

Farfalle with Tomatoes and Bocconcini

serves 4

2 tablespoons olive oil

1 teaspoon yellow asafetida powder

1 cup tomato purée

2 bay leaves

4 medium-sized, firm, ripe tomatoes, peeled, seeded
  and chopped

2 tablespoons butter

1 tablespoon sugar

1 teaspoon salt

½ teaspoon freshly-cracked black pepper

250g (½-pound) *farfalle* pasta

150g (5 ounces) fresh *bocconcini*, diced

3 tablespoons fresh basil leaves, chopped

extra whole basil leaves for garnish

Heat the olive oil in a medium-sized saucepan over
moderate heat. Add the asafetida and sauté momentarily.
Pour in the tomato purée and bay leaves, and simmer for
10 minutes or until the sauce is quite thick. Stir in the
chopped fresh tomatoes, the butter, sugar, salt and
pepper, and cook for 2 minutes more. The tomato pieces
should still be chunky. Remove from the heat, cover and
set the sauce aside.
Boil the pasta in plenty of salted water, according to the
instructions on the packet. Drain and keep warm.
Return the sauce to moderate heat. Fold the *bocconcini* into
the hot sauce. As the cheese starts to melt, fold in the
fresh basil.
Serve: Immediately divide the pasta onto warmed
serving plates, pour the sauce over the pasta, and garnish
with basil leaves.

This is a quick version of a succulent North Indian dish that my spiritual master,
Srila Prabhupada, taught his young disciple Yamuna Devi in 1966. Yamuna has gone
on to become one of the world's foremost authorities on vegetarian cuisine.

Chickpeas in Golden Karhi Sauce

serves 4

1 bay leaf

one small piece cinnamon stick

2 whole cardamom pods

5 tablespoons sifted chickpea flour

2½ cups water

2 cups yogurt or buttermilk

¾ teaspoon turmeric

2 teaspoons coriander powder

1 teaspoon salt

10 fresh curry leaves

2 tablespoons finely-chopped
  fresh coriander

3 cups cooked chickpeas

Seasoning

2 tablespoons ghee

2 teaspoons cumin seeds

2 small dried red chilies

Dry-roast the bay leaf, cinnamon and cardamom in a frying pan over moderate heat for 3 minutes, or until fragrant. Transfer to a mortar and pestle or spice grinder and reduce to a powder.

Whisk the chickpea flour in a bowl with a few tablespoons of the water to form a smooth batter. Gradually whisk in the rest of the water, the yogurt, turmeric, coriander powder, salt, curry leaves, half the fresh coriander and the dry-roasted spice powder.

Heat the mixture, stirring often, in a heavy saucepan over moderate heat. When it boils, reduce the heat slightly, and simmer for 10 minutes or until the sauce has thickened. Add the chickpeas, and simmer for another 2 minutes.

Season: Heat the ghee in a small saucepan over moderate heat. When fairly hot, drop in the cumin seeds and dried chili. Fry until the cumin seeds turn a rich brown colour. Pour the seasonings into the *karhi*, fold in the remaining fresh coriander.

Serve the chickpeas in *karhi* piping hot, accompanied with freshly cooked rice.

Plump, yellow Hokkien noodles have been described as the spaghetti of the noodle world — thick and succulent, with a substantial 'meatiness' to them.

Stir-fried Hokkien Noodles
with Asian Greens & Tofu

serves 4

500g (1 pound) eggless *Hokkien* noodles

2 tablespoons Chinese black beans, coarsely chopped (do not rinse)

¼ cup white grape juice or water

½ teaspoon yellow asafetida powder

1 tablespoon finely-chopped fresh ginger

1 teaspoon fresh red chili, seeded and finely chopped

¾ cup rich vegetable stock

2 tablespoons soy sauce

1 teaspoon sugar

1 teaspoon Chinese sesame oil

2½ tablespoons peanut oil

500g (1 pound) *choy sum*, or Chinese greens of your choice, trimmed

500g (1 pound) firm fresh tofu, cubed 2cm (¾-inch)

Place the noodles in a heatproof bowl, cover with boiling water and stand for 1 minute. Drain.

Soak the chopped black beans in the grape juice or water for 10 minutes, then drain and reserve the beans and liquid.

Mix together the drained beans, asafetida powder, ginger and fresh chili.

Combine the vegetable stock, soy sauce, sugar, sesame oil and reserved black bean soaking liquid.

Heat a large wok or frying pan until very hot, add 1 tablespoon peanut oil, and just before it starts to smoke, add the dry black bean mixture and stir over medium heat for 30 seconds, or until fragrant.

Add the *choy sum*, drained noodles and the liquid stock mixture, stir briefly, cover and simmer for 2 minutes, or until the greens are just wilted. Remove the lid, add the tofu, stir through carefully, and simmer for a further 2–3 minutes, uncovered, until the sauce is slightly reduced and the noodles are tender. If you want a less juicy dish, now stir a mixture of one tablespoon each of cornflour (cornstarch) and water.

Serve: Place the noodles in warm serving bowls and serve immediately.

Hokkien noodles started off as the favourite of the Hokkien Chinese, who introduced them to Malaysia where they play a major role in Malaysian hawker-style dishes, such as the well-known *mee goreng*. They're perfect for quick, easy stir-fries or soups , so it's good to have a packet in the fridge. They're generally sold vacuum-packed in plastic bags in the refrigerated section of Asian food stores or supermarkets.

Salads

The Chinese-Malay salad known as rojak is an example of a classic Indonesian dish (called rujak) that has hybridised somewhere else. This version tantalises the senses with a brilliant array of hot, sweet, sour and salty tastes, coupled with an assortment of juicy, slippery, leafy, crunchy, spongy and crispy textures. Really, it tastes as good as it sounds.

Malaysian Sweet, Sour & Hot Salad (Rojak)

serves 6

½ large ripe firm pineapple,
   cut into wedges
1 large green mango, peeled,
   seeded and cut into thin wedges
1 choko (*chayote*), peeled, sliced
   thinly and lightly salted
1 small yam bean (*jicama,
   bangkwang*), peeled and
   cut in wedges
2 Lebanese cucumbers, cut
   in wedges
100g (3 ounces) fried bean curd
   cubes, quartered
leaves from 1 bunch *kangkong*
   (water convolvulus), or
   1 bunch watercress
½ cup roasted peanuts, coarsely
   ground

Sauce

2 tablespoons tamarind pulp,
   reconstituted in 1 cup water
2 tablespoons *kechap manis*
   (sweet soy sauce)
2 teaspoons *sambal oelek*
1 teaspoon sweet chili sauce
1 tablespoon palm sugar, finely
   ground

Combine the sauce ingredients in a bowl and stir to dissolve the sugar.
Serve: Arrange the prepared fruits and vegetables, bean curd and *kangkong* leaves on a platter or in individual serving bowls. Drizzle over the sauce and sprinkle with the chopped peanuts. As an alternative, serve the sauce so diners can drizzle separately.

In traditional Indian cuisine, raita is the name given to a wide range of raw or semi-cooked fruit and vegetable salads. These simple, easy-to-prepare salads provide a light, cooling contrast to elaborately seasoned cooked preparations of the luncheon or evening meal. A raita generally features one or two main ingredients that float in lightly seasoned creamy fresh yogurt. Serve this raita in small bowls, allowing ½ cup per serving.

Spinach & Yogurt Salad (Palak Raita)

serves 6

375g (13 ounces) fresh spinach
1 teaspoon cumin seeds
2 cups natural yogurt, or 1½
   cups yogurt and ½ cup light
   sour cream
1 teaspoon salt
¼ teaspoon freshly-ground
   black pepper

Wash the spinach three times in successive changes of cold water. Sort out and remove the thick stems.

Steam the leaves in a small saucepan with a sprinkle of water for 10 minutes over low heat, or until the leaves are wilted and soft. Remove the spinach, cool slightly and press out the water.

Chop the spinach very finely.

Heat the cumin seeds in a small dry frying pan over low heat, tossing and roasting the seeds for about 5 minutes, or until lightly browned. Remove and crush them to a coarse powder.

Whisk the yogurt in a medium-sized bowl until creamy. Fold in the spinach, cumin, salt and pepper. Mix well.

Serve chilled.

Grilled Tempe & Mixed Leaves with Black Bean Dressing

serves 4

100g (4 ounces) snow peas

1 Lebanese cucumber

1 carrot, peeled

50g (2 ounces), about 1 packed cup *mesclun* (mixed salad leaves)

50g (2 ounces), about 1 packed cup rocket leaves

50g (2 ounces), about 1/3 cup chopped roasted peanuts

1/3 cup coriander leaves

oil for deep-frying

750g (1 1/2 pounds) *tempe*, cut into long thin slices

50g (2 ounces), about 2/3 cup snow pea sprouts

Dressing

2 tablespoons Chinese black beans

1/2 teaspoon yellow asafetida powder

2 teaspoons finely-grated fresh ginger

1 1/2 tablespoons soy sauce

1/2 teaspoons *sambal oelek*

1/4 cup olive oil

1 1/2 tablespoons freshly-squeezed lime juice

2 teaspoons palm sugar, finely-grated, or brown sugar

Soak the black beans in cold water for 10 minutes. Drain, rinse and chop finely.

Whisk the chopped beans with all the other dressing ingredients.

Blanch the snow peas in boiling water for 20 seconds, drain and refresh under cold running water, then cut into long thin strips.

Slice the cucumber and carrot into long thin strips by pressing firmly with a vegetable peeler.

Combine the snow peas, cucumber, carrot, salad leaves, rocket, peanuts and coriander, and toss gently to combine.

Heat the oil in a pan or wok and deep-fry the *tempe* slices until golden brown, then drain.

Serve: Place salad mixture on serving plates, top with sliced warm *tempe*, drizzle with dressing and scatter with snow pea sprouts.

Tempe is a cheesy substance made by soaking and boiling soya beans, inoculating them with a fungus *Rhizopus oligosporus*, packing them into thin slabs wrapped in polythene (or banana leaves pierced with holes) and leaving to ferment. *Tempe* is easily digested, delicious and a great source of protein, and best fried for optimum taste and texture.

With its hot pungent flavour, horseradish is a good counter-part to rich and oily foods, such as this warm potato salad. It's chock full of surprising tastes, colours and textures — aromatic fennel seeds, crunchy smoked almonds, pink-skinned potatoes, fresh dill and lovely green leaves of baby spinach, all coddled in a creamy mayonnaise laced with punch-in-the-nose horseradish.

Warm Potato Salad with Horseradish Mayonnaise

serves 6

750g (1 ½ pounds) Pink Eye potatoes cut into large chunks

3 teaspoons fennel seeds, dry roasted in a pan until aromatic

¾ cup chopped smoked almonds

3 cups baby spinach leaves, stalks removed

Dressing

²/₃ cup good eggless mayonnaise

¹/₃ cup sour cream

1 ½ tablespoons fresh dill, chopped

1 ½ teaspoons salt

1 teaspoon freshly-cracked black pepper

1 ½ tablespoons grated horseradish, prepared just before adding to the dressing

Combine all the dressing ingredients in the bowl set aside to serve the salad.

Boil the potatoes in a large saucepan of lightly salted water until tender. Drain them.

Fold the hot potatoes through the dressing while still hot, and set aside for 10 minutes.

Serve: Fold in the toasted fennel seeds, chopped almonds and baby spinach leaves. Serve immediately.

Leafy Butter Lettuce
with Pine Nuts & Pomegranate

This is a dynamic-looking salad combining leafy, pale green butter lettuce leaves with an emerald green chiffonade of spinach leaves. Golden pine nuts and ruby-red pomegranate seeds top off the visual experience.

serves 4

3 tablespoons pine nuts

12 large spinach leaves, stalks removed, rinsed, drained and trimmed

2 medium butter lettuces, or other leafy greens

2 tablespoons extra-virgin olive oil

½ teaspoon salt

¼ teaspoon freshly-ground black pepper

½ cup pomegranate seeds

2 tablespoons fresh lemon juice

Toast the pine nuts in a frying pan over low heat, stirring constantly until golden brown. Set aside.

Roll the spinach leaves into a tight log and slice them crosswise into a fine *chiffonade*. Combine the spinach and lettuce in a salad bowl.

Drizzle with oil, season with salt and pepper, and toss to mix.

Serve: Sprinkle the pomegranate seeds, pine nuts, and drizzle on the lemon juice. Serve immediately.

Sprouted Mung Bean Salad

Known as moong ki chat, this very popular salad is eaten as a road-side snack in India, especially in Delhi. The chili, lemon and tongue-tingling spice combination chat masala give it a pleasant bite. Home sprouted mung beans taste best.

serves 6

1 medium potato

1 small green chili, minced fine

1 tablespoon coriander leaves, chopped fine

250g (9 ounces) sprouted mung beans, about 1¾ cups — tender ones with tiny sprouts about

1.5cm (½-inch) are best

1 medium tomato, diced

1½ teaspoons *chat masala*, or more to taste

2 tablespoons lemon juice

1 teaspoon salt

Boil the potato until tender, peel and dice it.

Combine all the ingredients.

Serve immediately.

This mouth-watering salad from ancient times incorporated a resourceful way of using up stale Arab flat breads. Fattoush literally means 'wet bread', and traditionally the bread was soaked in water then toasted to revive it. My version of this recipe omits the soaking.

Lebanese Toasted Bread Salad (Fattoush)

serves 6

2 medium pita breads

1 small romaine or cos lettuce

8 pink radishes, quartered lengthwise

2 Lebanese cucumbers, peeled
  and sliced

4 large brine-pickled cucumbers, sliced

3 medium tomatoes, cut into eighths

½ cup finely-chopped, flat-leaf parsley

⅓ cup finely-chopped, fragrant
  mint leaves

¼ cup finely-shredded heart of
  iceberg lettuce

1 green chili, seeded and sliced
  fine julienne

Dressing

¼ cup fresh lemon juice

¼ cup extra-virgin olive oil

1 teaspoon yellow asafetida powder

1 teaspoon salt

Garnish

½ teaspoon freshly-ground black
  pepper

2 tablespoons coarsely ground sumac

Split each of the pita breads in half horizontally so that you have 4 thin rounds of bread.

Toast the breads lightly under a grill until just pale golden and crisp. Break up the toasted bread into small pieces and put in the bottom of a large salad bowl.

Pile the cut vegetables and herbs on top of the toasted bread.

Whisk together the dressing ingredients, and pour over the salad. Sprinkle with the pepper and *sumac*, and quickly toss the salad.

Serve immediately so the bread stays crisp.

A key ingredient in *fattoush* is *sumac*, a dark red, lemony astringent flavouring much used in Middle Eastern cuisine. *Sumac* is made from the dried red berries of the bush *Rhus coriara*, and is available in Middle Eastern shops. Note that you can use fresh or frozen and thawed Arab bread for this recipe. Traditional versions of this recipe use *melokhia* leaves, which are hard to come by. I have replaced them with romaine or cos lettuce.

A fabulous, warm, short-order winter salad with bold flavours and good looks.

Oven-roasted Cauliflower, Feta Cheese & Lentils

serves 4–6

1 large cauliflower cut into
    medium florets
¼ cup light olive oil
1 teaspoon sea salt
one 400g (14-ounce) can brown
    lentils, about 1ı cups, drained
250g (9 ounces) *feta* cheese cut
    into ½ inch cubes
1 cup stoned black olives,
    preferably *kalamata*
50g (2 ounces) watercress leaves
1 tablespoon balsamic vinegar
2 tablespoons extra-virgin olive oil
¼ teaspoon freshly-ground
    black pepper

Preheat the oven to 220°C/425°F.

Combine the cauliflower, light olive oil and salt in a large serving bowl, then transfer to a large deep tray or casserole.

Roast for about 20 minutes or until the cauliflower is slightly golden and cooked *al dente*. Return the hot, cooked cauliflower with any pan juices to the serving bowl.

Fold the cauliflower with the lentils, *feta* cheese, olives and watercress.

Whisk together the balsamic vinegar and extra-virgin olive oil and pour over the salad. Gently toss.

Serve immediately, with a grinding of black pepper.

Salade Niçoise

Traditional salade niçoise (pronounced nee-swahz), one of the great classic dishes from the south of France, was always served as a first course. The original version always contained anchovies, and later it was made more substantial with the addition of tuna. Here's my succulent vegetarian version.

serves 6

4 tablespoons extra-virgin olive oil

3 tablespoons freshly-squeezed lemon juice

500g (1 pound) small new potatoes

1 teaspoon salt

½ teaspoon freshly-ground black pepper

500g (1 pound) baby green beans, trimmed, steamed until tender and then refreshed

1 small red capsicum (pepper), sliced thinly

1 small green capsicum (pepper), sliced thinly

500g (1 pound) cherry tomatoes, halved

200g (6½ ounces) artichoke hearts

½ cup tiny *niçoise* olives, or other small black olives

2 tablespoons brine-packed capers

¾ packed cup small basil leaves, whole

2 tablespoons finely-chopped flat-leaf parsley

½ teaspoon yellow asafetida powder

leaves from one cos (romaine) lettuce

Mix half the oil with one third of the lemon juice.

Steam, peel and quarter the potatoes. Dress them with the lemon and oil while they are still warm, and sprinkle them with half the salt and pepper.

Combine the potatoes with the steamed beans, the capsicum slices, cherry tomatoes, the artichokes, olives, capers, basil and parsley in a large bowl.

Whisk together the remaining oil, lemon juice, salt, pepper and yellow asafetida powder.

Serve: Arrange the lettuce on a large serving platter. Combine the dressing with the salad vegetables and decoratively arrange them on the bed of lettuce. Serve immediately.

Tex-Mex Potato Salad

Served warm or chilled, this Latin-influenced American salad makes a spicy addition to any meal.

serves 6

1 kilo (2 pounds) small red-skinned
   potatoes
½ cup olive oil
1 teaspoon yellow asafetida powder
2 teaspoons salt
½ cup coriander leaves, chopped fine
1 cup grated sharp cheddar cheese

Tex-Mex Spices

1 teaspoon Spanish-style hot smoked
   paprika
1 tablespoon sweet paprika
½ cayenne pepper
2 teaspoons ground cumin seeds
2 teaspoons ground coriander
1 teaspoon white pepper

Simmer the potatoes whole in a large saucepan of lightly salted water for 15 minutes, or until they are just tender. Drain, allow them to cool briefly, then peel them. Slice thickly and transfer to a serving bowl.

Warm the olive oil in a frying pan over low heat. When the oil is fairly hot but not smoking, remove it from the heat, sprinkle in the yellow asafetida powder and sauté momentarily. Stir in the Tex-Mex spices, heat them through in the hot oil for a few seconds and quickly pour the mixture over the potatoes, tossing them gently. Add the salt, fresh coriander and the cheese. Combine well.

Serve the salad warm or at room temperature.

Salad of Vietnamese Greens

The beauty of this delicious salad is its simplicity.

serves 4

200g (7 ounces) bean sprouts
1 packed cup basil leaves
¾ packed cup Vietnamese
   mint leaves
¾ packed cup coriander leaves
2 fresh small red chilies, sliced
1 lime, quartered

Wash and thoroughly drain all the vegetables and herbs.
Combine all the ingredients.
Serve on 4 individual platters with a wedge of lime.

Note: Vietnamese mint is also known as *rau ram* (pronounced *row-ram*) and *laksa* leaf.

Savouries
& Finger Foods

Corn Cakes with Maple Syrup

Fancy something a little different for breakfast? Try these.

makes 10–12 pancakes

½ cup self-raising flour

1 cup fine polenta

½ teaspoon baking powder

1 cup milk

2 tablespoons sour cream

corn kernels from one large cooked
  corn cob, about 1 cup

1 teaspoon salt

½ teaspoon freshly-ground
  black pepper

4 or 5 tablespoons
  melted butter

1 cup maple syrup for serving

Combine the flour, polenta and baking powder in a large mixing bowl. Whisk in the milk, sour cream, corn kernels, salt and pepper. Allow the polenta to soak for 1 minute.

Heat a non-stick frying pan over moderate heat, drizzle in some of the melted butter, and fry ¼ cupfuls of the mixture on both sides for 3 or 4 minutes each side, or until golden brown.

Serve hot with the maple syrup.

The simplest recipes are often the most delicious. This is definitely true in the case of these shiny half-moons of pastry stuffed with lightly seasoned mashed potatoes. My quick version uses frozen wonton wrappers, available in well-stocked Asian shops. Serve vareneki hot with butter and sour cream.

Ukranian Potato Dumplings
(Vareneki)

makes 20–30 dumplings

3–4 tablespoons butter

½ teaspoon yellow asafetida powder

½ teaspoon dried dill

350g (12 ounces) potatoes, peeled, quartered, boiled until soft and mashed

1 teaspoon salt

½ teaspoon freshly-ground black pepper

30 frozen 8cm (3-inch) round wonton wrappers, thawed

2–3 tablespoons slightly burnt butter reserved for serving

sour cream for serving

Melt the butter in a small saucepan over moderate heat. Sprinkle in the yellow asafetida powder, and sauté momentarily. Remove from the heat and stir in the dill.

Combine the mashed potatoes with the flavoured butter, the salt and the pepper.

Fill: Separate all the wonton wrappers. Place 2 teaspoons of filling onto the middle of each wrapper. Dip your finger in some water and run it around the edge of the dough. Fold it over, making a half-moon shape. Pinch the edges together with your fingers or crimp with the teeth of a fork.

Drop a third of the *vareneki* into a very large saucepan of salted boiling water. Simmer, uncovered for about 2 minutes, or until the dumplings float to the surface. Carefully remove with a slotted spoon, and keep in a covered serving dish while you cook the rest.

Serve: Moisten with the reserved butter and serve with sour cream.

Note: *Vareneki* can be successfully reheated by frying them in butter.

Feta & Potato Spring Rolls
with Green Pea Chutney

Although it may seem an unlikely combination, herbed potato mixed with feta cheese and fried in crispy spring roll wrappers really does work incredibly well. And as far as the super-quick, super-quirky green pea chutney goes, that's also surprisingly delicious.

serves 4–6

600g (1¼ pounds) potatoes, peeled and cut into large chunks

4 tablespoons butter

200g (7 ounces) *feta* cheese, cut into tiny cubes

½–1 teaspoon salt, depending on the saltiness of the *feta*

1 teaspoon freshly-ground black pepper

1–2 tablespoons fresh mint, coriander or parsley, chopped

16 spring roll wrappers

1 teaspoon cornflour (cornstarch), made into a paste with a little cold water

oil for deep-frying

green pea chutney to serve (recipe follows)

Boil the potatoes in lightly salted water until soft. Mash them thoroughly with the butter, and fold in the *feta*, salt, pepper and herbs.

Divide the mixture into 16, and roll each portion into a log about 12cm (4½ inches) long. Place a log near the corner of a spring roll sheet.

Roll the sheet over the filling, tuck in the sides and roll up tightly. Seal the final corner with a dab of paste. Continue filling the remaining spring rolls. Heat the oil over moderate heat until fairly hot.

Deep-fry the spring rolls, turning once, for about 45 seconds or until lightly browned. Drain on paper towels.

Serve hot or warm with the green pea chutney.

Green Pea Chutney

Adapted from a recipe by Yamuna Devi from her award-winning book Yamuna's Table.

⅓ cup almonds, pan-toasted until golden, and chopped

1 cup frozen peas, defrosted

1 teaspoon grated fresh ginger

2–3 tablespoons water

2 teaspoons fresh lime juice

¼ cup fresh coriander leaves

1 teaspoon salt

½ teaspoon freshly-ground pepper

Pulse the toasted almonds in a food processor until finely minced.
Add the remaining ingredients and process until smooth. If you prefer a looser consistency, add a little more water and pulse again.
Serve with the spring rolls. Makes about 1¼ cups.

I was dubious when I was supplied this recipe for chili biscuits by a little old lady from Pasadena (seriously). She assured me they were delicious, and after cooking my first batch I had to agree.

Cheddar & Jalapeño Chili Biscuits

makes about 18 biscuits

1 cup plain flour

½ cup yellow cornmeal

2 teaspoons baking powder

½ teaspoon baking soda

½ teaspoon salt

2 tablespoons cold unsalted butter, cut into bits

1½ cups grated extra tasty cheddar cheese

2 pickled 4cm (1½-inch) *jalapeño* chilies, minced

2 fresh 4cm (1½-inch) *jalapeño* chilies, minced

²⁄₃ cup milk

Preheat the oven to 220°C/425°F.
Sift together the flour, cornmeal, baking powder, baking soda and salt in a bowl. Rub in the butter and combine thoroughly until the mixture resembles coarse meal.
Stir in the cheese and the chilies, add the milk and stir the mixture until it forms a soft and sticky dough.
Drop the dough by rounded tablespoons onto a buttered baking sheet.
Bake the biscuits in the centre of the preheated oven for 15–20 minutes, or until they are pale golden.
Serve at room temperature.

Jalapeño chilies (pronounced 'halapenyo') are the rounded, fleshy variety with a medium level of heat, 5.5 on the Richter Scale, sorry – the chili heat scale. They have become one of the most popular and versatile chilies around these days, and find their way into *salsas*, stews, salads, dressings and even biscuits.

If you love popcorn, you'll love these three variations.
We make buckets of the stuff in our house.

Savoury Popcorn

**each recipe makes
about 9 cups of popcorn**

Plain Popcorn

2 tablespoons vegetable oil

½ cup popcorn kernels

Heat the oil to almost smoking in a large, heavy bottomed pot over moderate heat.

Add the popping corn and shake the pan, loosely covered with a lid, for 3 or 4 minutes, or until you hear that the corn has popped. Alternatively, if you are using an electric corn popper or air popper, follow the manufacturer's directions. Pour the popcorn immediately into a bowl and sprinkle with salt.

Parmesan Popcorn

3 tablespoons butter

½ cup freshly-grated Parmesan cheese

9 cups cooked unsalted popcorn

Melt the butter in a small pan over moderate heat.

Serve: Drizzle the butter over the cooked popcorn in a large bowl. Sprinkle the Parmesan cheese over the popcorn, tossing it, and season with salt if desired.

Chinese-flavoured Sesame Popcorn

3 tablespoons butter

1 teaspoon soy sauce

1 tablespoon Chinese sesame oil

9 cups cooked unsalted popcorn

Melt the butter with the soy sauce in a small pan over moderate heat. Stir in the sesame oil.

Serve: Drizzle the mixture over the cooked popcorn in a large bowl. Season with salt if required.

Hot Chili Popcorn

3 tablespoons unsalted butter

1 teaspoon Tabasco

½ teaspoon salt

¼ teaspoon cayenne pepper, or to taste

9 cups cooked unsalted popcorn

Melt the butter with the Tabasco in a small pan over moderate heat.

Serve: Drizzle the mixture over the cooked popcorn in a large bowl, tossing it well. Combine the salt and cayenne. Toss the mixture through the popcorn.

Koftas in Tomato Sauce

Koftas are succulent, Indian-style vegetable balls that can be served soaking in sauce or smothered in gravy. A number of vegetables are suitable for making kofta – potato, cabbage, cauliflower, spinach and radish are the most popular. My favourite koftas are made from a mixture of cauliflower and cabbage.

makes 24 *koftas*

Sauce

2 tablespoons olive oil

1 tablespoon butter

2 bay leaves

½ teaspoon yellow asafetida powder

4 cups tomato purée

1 teaspoon dried basil

2 teaspoons salt

¼ teaspoon freshly-ground black pepper

1½ teaspoons sugar

Koftas

2 cups grated cauliflower

2 cups grated cabbage

1½ cups chickpea flour

½ teaspoon yellow asafetida powder

1 teaspoon ground cumin

1½ teaspoon salt

1 teaspoon *garam masala*

½ teaspoon cayenne

ghee or oil for deep frying

The sauce

Heat the oil and butter together in a saucepan over moderate heat. When hot, drop in the bay leaves and sauté for 1 minute or until fragrant. Sprinkle in the yellow asafetida powder, and fry momentarily.

Stir in the tomato purée and basil. Raise the heat, bring to the boil, reduce the heat and simmer for 10 minutes or until a little reduced.

Add in the salt, pepper and sugar, remove from the heat and keep warm.

The koftas

Combine all the *kofta* ingredients in a bowl until well mixed. Roll the mixture into 24 balls. Heat the ghee or oil for deep-frying in a wok or deep pan over fairly high heat to about 180°C/350°F. Carefully drop in 6–8 balls.

Fry the *koftas* for 2–3 minutes or until they rise to the surface and start to colour. Reduce the heat to low, and fry for another 8–10 minutes, or until they are a deep reddish brown. Remove and drain on paper towels. Reheat the oil to its original temperature, and repeat the frying procedure for the remaining batches of *koftas*.

Serve: Soak the *koftas* in the hot sauce 10 minutes before serving time to allow them to fully soak and become plump and succulent. They are great on a bed of steaming hot Thai rice as part of a main meal. They also work well as an accompaniment.

Cheesy Bean & Tortilla Stacks (Tostadas)

A popular Mexican combination — a stack of 're-fried' beans — frijoles refritos — (pronounced free-whole-ess ref-ree-toss), crispy lettuce, guacamole, sour cream, spicy sauce and cheese piled onto a crispy fried corn tortilla. Don't even dream of not making a mess — serve with plenty of napkins!

makes 6 *tostadas*

6 large corn tortillas

oil for deep frying

frijoles refritos (recipe follows)

4 medium tomatoes, chopped or
cut into thin wedges

2 cups shredded iceberg lettuce

2 ripe, medium avocados, mashed
with a little salt, pepper and
lemon, or guacamole (recipe
follows)

¼ to ½ cup sour cream

spicy tomato sauce (recipe follows)

1 cup grated tasty cheddar cheese

Guacamole

2 ripe medium avocados, peeled,
stoned and mashed

2 tablespoons finely-shredded
iceberg lettuce leaves

1 or 2 small green chilies, seeded
and finely chopped

2 teaspoons fresh lemon or
lime juice

¼ teaspoon yellow asafetida
powder

½ teaspoon salt

¼ teaspoon freshly-ground
black pepper

Combine all the ingredients.

Heat sufficient oil in a frying pan to pan-fry the tortillas. When the oil is hot, drop in a tortilla.

Fry it until golden brown on both sides. Remove from the oil with tongs, shake off any excess oil, and while still hot press into a bowl to produce a shallow cup shape. Remove when firm. Repeat for all the tortillas.

Stack the tortillas as follows: A layer of *frijoles refritos*, some tomato pieces, shredded lettuce, a spoon of avocado or guacamole next to a dollop of sour cream, a large spoonful of tomato sauce, and a generous pile of grated cheese.
Serve immediately.

'Refried' Beans (frijoles refritos)

2 tablespoons butter

¼ teaspoon yellow asafetida
powder

2 cups cooked pinto or red kidney
beans

1 teaspoon chili powder or less to
taste

½ teaspoon cumin powder

½ teaspoon salt

Heat the butter in a frying pan over moderately high heat. Sprinkle in the yellow asafetida powder, stir in half the beans, a few tablespoons water, the chili powder, cumin and salt.
Fry the beans until they start to stick to the pan, and partially mash the beans with a masher.
Add the rest of the beans and a little more water. Continue frying, scraping the pan to prevent sticking and incorporating all the beans. When the beans are a thick chunky paste, remove from the heat.

Spicy Tomato Sauce

1 tablespoon olive oil

1 teaspoon green chili, seeded and
minced

¼ teaspoon yellow asafetida
powder

1 teaspoon chili powder, or less to
taste

1 cup tomato purée

½ teaspoon lemon juice

½ teaspoon salt

1 teaspoon sugar

Heat the oil in a small saucepan over moderate heat. Sprinkle in the green chili, sauté for 30 seconds, sprinkle in the yellow asafetida powder, chili powder and tomato purée, bring to the boil, then reduce to a simmer.
Cook the sauce uncovered for 5 minutes, or until somewhat reduced. Add the lemon juice, salt and sugar and remove from the heat.

Malaysian Curry Puffs
with Quick Tamarind Chutney

Our recipe-testing crew (and miscellaneous hangers-on) polished off these delicacies in record time. If you're looking for a finger food par excellence, seek no further.

makes about 40 bite-size puffs

1 cup sweet potato, diced very small

1 cup carrot, diced very small

1 cup potato, diced very small

1 cup peas

2 tablespoons ghee or oil

fresh curry leaves from 3 large sprigs,
    torn

1 tablespoon grated fresh ginger

½ teaspoon yellow asafetida powder

2 tablespoons Malaysian hot curry
    powder

2 teaspoons sugar

1 teaspoon salt

5 sheets ready-made puff pastry

ghee or oil for deep frying

quick tamarind chutney, to serve
    (recipe follows)

The filling
Steam the vegetables separately until tender. Drain.

Heat the ghee or oil in a frying pan over moderate heat. When the oil is hot, drop in the curry leaves and fry until they crackle, sprinkle in the ginger, fry for 1 minute or until aromatic, then add the yellow asafetida powder and fry momentarily.

Stir in the curry powder, all the cooked vegetables, the sugar and the salt. Fry together for 1 or 2 minutes then remove from the heat. Allow the mixture to cool.

The puffs
Cut the sheets of puff pastry into 8cm (3-inch) rounds with a pastry cutter.

Place 2 teaspoons of cooled filling in the centre of each square. Fold into semicircles and seal, leaving the edge plain, pressed with fork tines, or with a decorative pinched and fluted edge.

Heat the ghee or oil for deep-frying in a wok or deep frying pan over moderate heat until fairly hot.

Fry the puffs in batches for 2–3 minutes or until puffed and golden brown. Remove and drain on paper towels.

Serve hot, warm or cold with the accompanying tamarind chutney or sweet chili sauce.

Quick Tamarind Chutney

¼ cup dried tamarind, soaked in 2
    cups boiling water for ½ hour

½ teaspoon ground cumin

2 teaspoons ginger juice (juice
    squeezed from about 2
    tablespoons shredded ginger)

3 tablespoons brown sugar

½ teaspoon salt

big pinch chili powder

Pour the soaked tamarind through a sieve, collecting all the juice. Rub and squeeze the remaining pulp to extract all the tamarind purée. Discard the dry residue.

Combine the tamarind purée with all the remaining ingredients in a medium saucepan. Cook over moderately high heat for 10–15 minutes, or until reduced by half. Serve at room temperature. Makes 1 cup chutney.

Soft Vietnamese Spring Rolls
with Peanut Dipping Sauce

These very light and healthy uncooked finger foods are my version of the famous
soft Vietnamese spring rolls known as cha gio. Unlike their crispy deep-fried counterparts,
the wrappers for these soft, semi-transparent rolls require no cooking. The wrappers
are made from rice paper, known as banh trang, which needs only to be dipped in hot
water for a few moments before being filled.

makes 24 rolls

200g (7 ounces) finely-sliced strips
   of lettuce

200g (7 ounces) carrots, sliced into
   long slender julienne

200g (7 ounces) hard-fried tofu,
   sliced into slender strips

200g (7 ounces) bean sprouts

3 tablespoons coarsely-shredded
   mint leaves

3 tablespoons coarsely-shredded
   Vietnamese mint (*rau ram*)

3 tablespoons chopped roasted
   peanuts

1 tablespoon soy sauce

24 sheets *banh trang*

peanut dipping sauce
   (recipe follows)

Combine all the ingredients (except the *banh trang* wrappers and dipping sauce) in a large bowl until well mixed. Divide into 24 portions.

Dip one sheet of *banh trang* into a bowl of warm water. Leave in the water for a few seconds until soft and pliable, then remove, shake off the excess water, and lay the sheet on a clean, dry, work surface.

Pile one portion of filling in a line near the bottom of the wrapper, about 2.5cm (1 inch) from the edge and the same distance from each side.

Roll into a tight cigar, tucking in the sides half way. Seal the roll tightly—the sticky rice paper will adhere to itself without difficulty. Repeat for all the spring rolls.

Serve, arranged on a platter with the dipping sauce.

Banh trang wrappers, Vietnamese mint, and hard, fried tofu are available in well-stocked Asian grocers.

Peanut Dipping Sauce

4 tablespoons peanut butter

5 tablespoons soy sauce

3 tablespoons warm water

2 teaspoons sugar

1 teaspoon lemon juice

1 tablespoon coarsely-chopped
   roasted unsalted peanuts

1–2 teaspoons finely sliced red
   chilies.

Whisk together all the ingredients except the chopped peanuts and the sliced red chilies. Add a little water if necessary to make a sauce of dipping consistency. Transfer the sauce to a small serving bowl and sprinkle with the chopped peanuts. Place the chili slices on a small dish.

Serve as an accompaniment to the spring rolls and sauce.

Crispy Batter-fried Vegetables (Pakoras)

Here's a couple of varieties of pakora — whole chilies and cauliflower, in different batters —
with accompanying uncooked chutneys.

Cauliflower Pakoras with Fresh Mint Chutney

¾ cup chickpea flour

¼ cup cornflour (cornstarch)

½ teaspoon baking powder

1 teaspoon cayenne pepper

1 teaspoon yellow asafetida powder

½ teaspoon turmeric

1½ teaspoons salt

1 tablespoon olive oil

up to ½ cup water

ghee or oil for deep-frying

½ large cauliflower cut into
   approximately 30 small florets

Fresh Mint Chutney

1 tablespoon lime juice

1 tablespoon orange juice

1 tablespoon maple syrup

¾ cup fresh mint leaves

1 small green chili, chopped

2 tablespoons fresh or dried coconut

½ teaspoon salt

Whisk together the two flours, baking powder, cayenne, asafetida, turmeric and salt. Pour in the tablespoon of olive oil and whisk in sufficient water to form a smooth batter, the consistency of medium-thin cream.

Heat the ghee or oil for deep-frying in a wok or deep frying pan. When the oil is hot, dip 6 or 8 cauliflower pieces in the batter and lower into the hot oil.

Deep-fry the cauliflower pieces for 3–4 minutes or until they are crisp and golden brown. Remove, drain on paper towels, and repeat for the rest of the cauliflower pieces.

For the fresh mint chutney: Combine all the ingredients in a food processor and blend until fully blended. Transfer to a serving dish.

Serve the *pakoras* hot accompanied by the fresh mint chutney. Makes about 30 *pakoras*.

The tradition of frying vegetables in batter is popular throughout the culinary world. In Italy, there's the delicious Neapolitan fritters known as *pasta cresciuta*, with ingredients like sundried tomato halves, zucchini flowers and sage leaves dipped in a yeasted batter and fried in olive oil. The Japanese dip all sorts of things, including zucchini, eggplant and carrot into a light thin batter and serve the *tempura* with dipping sauce.

In India, *pakoras* are almost a national passion. Cooked on bustling street corners, in snack houses and at home, the fritters are always served piping hot, usually with an accompanying sauce or chutney. The vegetables can be cut into rounds, sticks, fan shapes or slices. The varieties are endless.

Whole Fresh Green Chili Pakoras with Cooling Lime Yogurt

½ cup sifted chickpea flour

¼ cup cornflour (cornstarch)

½ teaspoon baking powder

1½ teaspoons *nigella (kalonji)* seeds

½ teaspoon turmeric

½ teaspoon yellow asafetida powder

1½ teaspoons salt

1 tablespoon olive oil

about ½ cup iced water

ghee or oil for deep frying

24 whole fresh green chilies, with stalks

Cooling Lime Yogurt

1¼ cups Greek-style yogurt

½ teaspoon freshly-grated lime zest

1 tablespoon fresh lime juice

Whisk together the 2 flours, baking powder, *nigella* seeds, turmeric, asafetida powder and salt. Pour in the tablespoon of olive oil and whisk in sufficient iced water to form a smooth batter, the consistency of medium-thin cream.

Heat the ghee or oil for deep-frying in a wok or deep frying pan over moderate heat until fairly hot.

Dip 6 or 8 chilies in the batter while holding the stalks, and lower into the hot oil.

Deep-fry the chilies for 3–4 minutes, or until they are crisp and golden brown. Remove, drain on paper towels, and repeat for all the chilies.

For the cooling lime yogurt: Whisk together the ingredients in a small serving bowl.

Serve the *pakoras* hot accompanied by the lime yogurt. Makes 24 *pakoras*.

Vegetable Turnovers (Calzone) with Red Pepper Sauce

Calzone (pronounced 'cal-zone-ay') are pockets of yeasted bread dough rolled out and filled with cheesy bits and baked in the oven or fried. My quick vegetarian version of these famous Italian turnovers is baked in puff-pastry or short-crust pastry. Red pepper sauce is a perfect accompaniment.

makes 16 *calzone*

1 cup fresh ricotta cheese, drained

½ cup grated mozzarella cheese

¼ cup tasty cheddar cheese

¼ cup dry breadcrumbs

½ cup chopped marinated
   eggplant, drained

½ cup coarsely-chopped
   black olives

2 tablespoons drained, brine-
   packed capers

½ cup chopped fresh basil leaves

¼ cup chopped, well-drained,
   oil-packed sundried tomatoes

2 tablespoons tomato paste

1 teaspoon salt

1 teaspoon sugar

4 sheets frozen puff-pastry or
   short-crust pastry

red pepper sauce (recipe follows)

Preheat the oven to 180°C/350°F.

The filling: Combine all the ingredients (except the pastry and red pepper sauce) in a bowl, mixing well to combine. Divide the filling into 16.

The pastry: Thaw the pastry, and with a 12cm (4½-inch) cutter, cut out 16 discs of pastry.

The *calzone*: Place a portion of filling in the centre of each pastry disc. Fold the pastry over to make a semicircle, enclosing the filling, but being careful to keep a 1cm (½-inch) border of pastry. Seal the pastry with a little water and press the edges together firmly. If you like, press with the tines of a fork or seal with a decorative, fluted edge.

Bake the pastries on a tray lined with baking paper in the centre of the oven for 20–25 minutes, or until the *calzone* are puffed and golden. Remove and cool slightly.

Serve the *calzone* warm, along with the red pepper sauce.

Red Pepper Sauce

4 large red capsicums (peppers),
   roasted, peeled
   and coarsely chopped

1 tablespoon avocado or olive oil

1 teaspoon salt

¼ teaspoon freshly-ground black
   pepper

¼ teaspoon cayenne pepper

Process the peppers in a food processor to form a chunky paste. Continue to process while drizzling in the oil. Add the salt, black pepper and cayenne, and ¼ cup water, or more, to form a saucy consistency. Remove and serve with the *calzone*. Makes about 1¼ cups.

Note: As an alternative to marinated eggplant, try grilling, pan-frying or deep-frying one small chopped eggplant.

This delectable thyme-scented tart is filled with spinach and three types of cheese: ricotta, feta and Swiss. Using a good quality, ready-made puff pastry ensures trouble-free, quick preparation time. This tart is also excellent served cold for picnics.

Spinach & Cheese Tart

makes one 20cm (8-inch) tart

1 cup ricotta cheese

½ cup *feta* cheese, chopped

1¼ cups dry breadcrumbs

220g (7 ounces) spinach leaves, blanched, chopped and drained

leaves from 2 or 3 stalks of thyme

1 teaspoon salt

½ teaspoon freshly-ground black pepper

¼ teaspoon freshly-grated nutmeg

1½ sheets ready-made puff pastry

½ cup grated Swiss cheese

2 or 3 firm ripe tomatoes, sliced

½ teaspoon sugar

Preheat the oven to 230°C/450°F.

Combine the ricotta, *feta*, breadcrumbs, spinach leaves, thyme, salt, pepper and nutmeg in a bowl. Mix well.

Line the base and sides of a 20cm (8-inch) tart tin with the puff pastry and prick the base with a fork.

Spoon the mixture into the pastry case, spreading the mixture evenly over the base.

Sprinkle with the grated Swiss cheese and cover with a single layer of tomato slices. Sprinkle the tomato with the sugar.

Bake in the preheated oven for about 25 minutes, or until the the cheese is browned and bubbling and the pastry is golden.

Serve hot or at room temperature.

Rosti Pancakes filled with Swiss Cheese & Tomatoes

In Switzerland, golden brown, flavourful potato pancakes called rosti have been enjoyed for generations. Served plain, these tempting pancakes are a perfect side dish. This version, filled with Gruyere or Emmental cheese and slices of tomato make a delightful breakfast, brunch or light luncheon dish.

makes 8 *rosti*

8 medium baking potatoes

¾ cup olive oil

4 tablespoons unsalted butter

salt and freshly-ground black pepper to taste

3 or 4 tomatoes, peeled and thinly sliced

²/₃ cup grated Swiss cheese

Boil the whole unpeeled potatoes in a large saucepan of lightly salted water over moderate heat for about 15 minutes, or until a skewer or knifepoint easily pierces the outer 1.5cm (½-inch) of potato but meets resistance in the centre. Drain, rinse under cold running water, and if possible refrigerate until well chilled. Peel the potatoes.

Shred the potatoes lengthwise to form long, even shreds in a food processor fitted with a large shredder blade, or on the large holes of a hand grater. Don't rinse away the starch. Divide the mixture into 8.

Heat 1 tablespoon of olive oil in a heavy 20cm (8-inch) frying pan over high heat until almost smoking.

Sprinkle in one portion of potato into the frying pan. Season lightly with salt and pepper. Quickly push any stray shreds from the outer rim of the pan to form an even, round pancake. Lightly press the top of the *rosti*. Reduce the heat to moderately high.

Fry the *rosti*, shaking and rotating the pan occasionally to loosen the potatoes, for about 3 minutes, or until well browned on the bottom. Add a couple of teaspoons of butter to the edge of the pan.

Flip the *rosti* over, or turn with a wide spatula. Season lightly again with salt and pepper, top with a few slices of tomato, and sprinkle with a couple of tablespoons of Swiss cheese. Continue cooking the *rosti* over moderately high heat, adding additional butter if the pan becomes dry, for another 3 minutes, or until browned on the second side.

Carefully fold the fully cooked *rosti* in half to enclose the cheese and tomatoes. Keep it warm while you cook the other *rosti*.

Serve warm or hot.

Rosti Tips

- Shredding the potatoes with a food processor gives the shreds a rounder shape and the pancakes a better texture.
- Be sure to use starchy baking potatoes. The starchiness is needed to bind the shreds of potato.
- Parboil the whole potatoes well ahead of time. Refrigerate for at least several hours before peeling and shredding.
- Add the potatoes when the oil in the pan is very hot and is almost smoking.
- Listen for a soft scraping noise as you shake the pan. When you hear it, you will know the *rosti* is browned and crisp.
- Cooking two *rosti* at a time using two frying pans halves the cooking time.
- *Rosti* may be held for a short while in a warm oven, but they're best served as soon as possible after cooking.

Breads
& Sandwiches

Grilled Vegetables Wrapped in Pita Breads (Souvlakia)

Souvlaki is a well-known grilled meat dish from Greece that is sometimes served wrapped in flatbreads. Here's a vegetarian version.

makes 8 *souvlakia*

4 long thin eggplants, cut into 2cm (¾-inch) rounds

2 medium zucchinis, cut into 2cm (¾-inch) rounds

8 firm plum tomatoes, cut in half lengthways, seeds squeezed out

1 large green capsicum (pepper), cut into 12 pieces

1 large red capsicum (pepper), cut into 12 pieces

Marinade

1 teaspoon yellow asafetida powder

⅓ cup olive oil

2 tablespoons balsamic vinegar, or lemon juice

1 teaspoon dried oregano or thyme

2 teaspoons salt

1 teaspoon freshly-ground black pepper

Sauce

1 cup Greek yogurt, preferably drained overnight

1 tablespoon olive oil

½ teaspoon yellow asafetida powder

½ teaspoon salt

¼ teaspoon freshly-ground black pepper

1 teaspoon sweet paprika

extra 2 tablespoons olive oil

8 pita breads

Combine all the cut vegetables in a large bowl. Whisk the marinade ingredients together in a small bowl, and pour the marinade over the vegetables. Toss and leave for 10 minutes.

Preheat a grill to very hot. Slide the vegetables alternatively onto 8 skewers. Brush with the marinade.

Grill them about 10cm (4 inches) from the heat, turning when required, for about 10 minutes, or until the vegetables are well browned and tender.

Whisk together all the sauce ingredients except for the paprika.

Brush the pita breads with 2 tablespoons olive oil. Heat the breads by wrapping them in a tea towel and placing them in a hot oven.

Remove the skewered vegetables from the grill. Unwrap the stack of breads and place one skewer of vegetables near the bottom of the top flatbread. Pull out the skewer, and place a dollop of sauce on top, followed by a drizzle of the marinade and a sprinkle of paprika.

Roll up the *souvlaki* and secure with a toothpick, or wrap in wax paper. Repeat for the remaining *souvlakia*.

Serve immediately.

Note: If using wooden skewers, be sure to soak them in water for ½ hour first to avoid them catching fire.

Open-faced Sandwich
of Pears & Gorgonzola

Blue cheeses, particularly the Italian gorgonzola dolce latte, have a special affinity
with pears and apples. If gorgonzola is too strong for your taste, try a milder blue cheese.

serves 4

125g (4 ounces) cream cheese

60g (2 ounces) gorgonzola *dolce
latte*, or blue cheese of
your choice

little milk or cream

chopped chervil leaves and
additional sprigs for garnish

freshly-ground black pepper

4 large squares Turkish bread, or
bread of your choice

2 ripe pears, thinly sliced

Combine the cream cheese and gorgonzola, adding a little milk or cream
to make a soft paste that's easy to spread.

Add the chopped chervil and season with pepper. Lightly toast the bread
or leave it untoasted, as you prefer.

Spread the cheese neatly over the top, then cover the cheese with over-
lapping slices of pear.

Serve garnished with additional sprigs of chervil.

Note: Juicy, buttery-fleshed pears are wonderful, but the Asian pear *nashi*,
which is at once juicy and crisp, is also excellent. The flesh is more granular
and less buttery, but it certainly adds a wonderful textural contrast to the
soft cheese.

If the skins on the pears are firm and smooth, leave the pears unpeeled.
On an open-faced sandwich the red, russet and golden skins of the pears
make a beautiful garnish in themselves. A squeeze of lemon on the pears
will certainly stop them browning, but will add an assertive taste that will
spoil the subtle mix of the cheese and pears, so try to assemble the sandwiches just before you serve them.

Toasted Focaccia with Hoummos & Moroccan Broad Bean Purée

The broad bean dip known in Morocco as bissara is so delicious that you better have some extra broad beans on hand to make more. The famous chickpea and sesame paste dip hoummos needs hardly any introduction. Delicious chunks of fresh focaccia are the perfect thing for scooping up these humble but heavenly foods. Happy dipping!

serves 6

2 medium *focaccia*, cut into wedges
   or chunks and toasted
chickpea dip (recipe follows)
broad bean purée (recipe follows)

Chickpea Dip (Hoummos)

1¼ cups cooked chickpeas
½ cup *tahini*
2 tablespoons lemon juice
¼ teaspoon yellow asafetida powder
little water
1 tablespoon olive oil for garnish
¼ teaspoon paprika for garnish
1 teaspoon chopped parsley for garnish

Process the chickpeas, *tahini*, lemon juice and yellow asafetida powder in a food processor until smooth, adding a little water if required for a purée consistency. Transfer to a serving bowl.

Serve at room temperature garnished with olive oil, paprika and parsley accompanied by chunks of toasted *focaccia*. Makes 1¼ cups.

Moroccan Broad Bean Purée

500g (1 pound) frozen broad beans, or 1kg (2 pounds)
   fresh broad beans, weighed before removing from
   their long pods
1½ tablespoons lemon juice
½ teaspoon yellow asafetida powder
¼ teaspoon salt
1 small green chili, seeded and chopped
2 tablespoons extra-virgin olive oil
sweet paprika for dusting
more olive oil for dusting
olives and salad greens to serve (optional)

Drop the frozen broad beans into a saucepan of lightly salted water. When the water returns to the boil, cook for 3 minutes, then remove, drain and refresh the bread buns with cold water. If using fresh broad beans, cook for 10 minutes or until tender.

Remove the skins from the beans revealing the bright green beans inside—this is fiddly but necessary.

Process the beans in a food processor along with the lemon juice, asafetida powder, salt, chili and olive oil. Transfer to a serving bowl.

Serve with a drizzle of olive oil and a dusting of paprika powder accompanied by the toasted *focaccia*, a bowl of olives, and a handful of baby salad greens dressed with extra-virgin olive oil and lemon juice.

Buttermilk Soda Bread

This recipe has never let me down. If you want a fast and easy homemade bread recipe with a good texture and a delicious tangy flavour, this is the one for you. Because it contains no yeast, this bread is best made and consumed on the same day.

makes 1 loaf

2 cups, about 300g (11 ounces) unbleached plain flour

2 cups, about 300g (11 ounces) wholemeal (whole wheat) plain flour

½ teaspoon cream of tartar

1 teaspoon bicarbonate of soda

1 teaspoon sea salt

2 cups buttermilk

sea salt flakes

Preheat the oven to 220°C/425°F. Lightly flour a baking tray.

Sift the flours, cream of tartar, bicarbonate of soda and sea salt into a large bowl. Make a well in the centre of the mixture.

Pour in almost all the buttermilk, then stir with a wooden spoon until thoroughly combined. Feel the dough. It should be slightly sticky. If too dry, add the remaining buttermilk. Transfer the dough to a lightly floured work surface.

Gently knead the dough for 1 minute (do not over knead).

Shape the dough into a round and place on the prepared baking tray. Cut a 1.5cm (½-inch) deep cross into the dough and sprinkle with the sea salt flakes.

Bake in the preheated oven for 30 minutes, or until golden and cooked through (test with a wooden skewer—if it comes out clean, it's done).

Remove from the oven and transfer to a wire rack. Allow to cool then cover with a dampened towel until required.

Serve: Break off chunks or cut into slices.

Cumin-flavoured
Grilled Triple-cheese Sandwich

Cumin seeds are well suited to cheese dishes. Here they are dry-roasted to flavour a combination of toasted multigrain bread with Parmesan, feta, Swiss cheese, and baby spinach—a selection that should satisfy the most discerning toasted cheese sandwich aficionado.

serves 4

8 slices multigrain wholemeal bread
butter
1 teaspoon cumin seeds, dry-
    roasted in a pan until aromatic
50g (1½ ounces) baby spinach
    leaves
60g (2 ounces) Gruyere or other
    Swiss cheese, shredded
30g Parmesan cheese, shredded
60g (2 ounces) *feta* cheese,
    crumbled or chopped finely
Freshly-ground black pepper

Butter all the bread, sprinkle half the slices with cumin seeds and half of the baby spinach leaves.

Cover the spinach with a combination of the Gruyere and Parmesan cheese, and top with the *feta* cheese and generous grindings of black pepper. Top with the remaining spinach leaves and the rest of the bread. Grill in a sandwich press until the bread is well toasted and the cheese melted.

Serve: Cut the sandwiches in half and serve immediately.

Avocados on Rye with Lime & Watercress

This combination is simple yet sublime.

makes 4 open-faced sandwiches

4 slices sourdough rye bread
unsalted butter
2 or 3 ripe avocados
1 lime
salt
freshly-ground black pepper
watercress or coriander leaves

Spread the bread with butter, cover with slices of avocado, and sprinkle with lime juice, salt and plenty of pepper.

Serve topped with watercress or coriander leaves.

Bruschetta are lightly toasted thick slices of bread seasoned and sprinkled with olive oil. Our test kitchen crew called this magnificent meal-in-itself 'the mother of all sandwiches'.

Bruschetta of Grilled Vegetables, Mozzarella & Pesto

serves 4

Vegetables

1 large red capsicum (pepper)

1 large green capsicum (pepper)

1 large eggplant cut into 1cm
  (½-inch) slices

2 zucchinis cut lengthwise into
  1cm (½-inch) slices

½ cup virgin olive oil, warmed
  through with leaves from 1 large
  sprig rosemary

salt and pepper

250g (½ pound) good
  quality *pesto*

4 roma tomatoes

Bread

4 slices sourdough bread 1cm
  (½-inch) thick

To serve

125g (4 ounces) mixed baby green
  leaves *(mesclun)*

300g (10 ounces) fresh buffalo
  mozzarella

handful basil leaves

The vegetables

Grill the peppers under a hot grill until the skins are blackened and charred. Seal in a plastic bag to sweat, then peel, cut into quarters or thick strips, and remove the seeds and membranes. Keep warm.

Brush the eggplant and zucchini with some of the rosemary infused oil and cook on a stove top grill until slightly charred but not limp. Season with salt and pepper.

Combine all the grilled vegetables with three-quarters of the *pesto* while they are still warm, and set aside in a warm place.

Slice the tomatoes and set them aside.

The bread: Liberally brush both sides of the bread slices with some of the rosemary infused olive oil and grill lightly on both sides.

Serve: Arrange the salad leaves on each plate and place the grilled bread on top. Arrange the grilled vegetable and sliced tomato over the bread and top with sliced mozzarella. Drizzle each with the remaining *pesto* and scatter basil leaves over.

Poached Strawberries
& Goat's Cheese on Toasted Baguette

Strawberries on toast! It may sound odd, but it's actually very delicious. Strawberries poached in orange juice with soft goat's cheese on top of toasted rounds of baguette makes a wonderful cocktail party appetizer.

makes 10 appetizer portions

10 large ripe strawberries, hulled
juice from 1 orange
1 teaspoon sugar
¼ teaspoon balsamic vinegar
   (optional)
½ large *baguette*, sliced and grilled
150g (5 ounces) soft goat's cheese
black pepper

Poach the strawberries with the orange juice, sugar and balsamic vinegar in a small saucepan over low heat for 3–4 minutes or until plump and tender. Drain.

Spread the grilled *baguette* slices with the soft goat's cheese, and top with a poached strawberry.

Serve with a generous grinding of black pepper.

Lavash Bread
with Hot & Sweet Pear Chutney

In accordance with Persian tradition, breads are served to accompany other things rather than a food to be enjoyed for its own sake. Toasted, crispy lavash is a perfect match for my wonderful carame anise-flavoured pear chutney.

serves 6

12 pieces crisp lavash bread, or
more according to taste
pear chutney (recipe follows)

Serve the crispy *lavash* accompanied with the room temperature chutney as an appetizer, or serve it either at the end of a meal instead of dessert or after dessert.

Pear Chutney

I formulated this delicious recipe in our test kitchen using Packham pears, with stunning results. Coupled with fennel seeds, it's a match made in heaven.

makes about 1½ cups

1½ tablespoons ghee

1½ teaspoons cumin seeds

1½ teaspoons fennel seeds

2 small green chilies, sliced into
thin rings

2 teaspoons minced fresh ginger

1 teaspoon turmeric

500g (1 pound) firm ripe pears

½ teaspoon cinnamon powder

½ teaspoon freshly-ground
nutmeg powder

¾ cup sugar

Heat the ghee in a heavy saucepan over moderate heat. Sprinkle in the cumin and fennel seeds, and sauté until a few shades darker and aromatic. Drop in the chilies and ginger and fry for about 1 minute, or until aromatic.

Add the turmeric and pears and stir together for a few minutes. Stir in the cinnamon and nutmeg. Reduce the heat slightly. If the mixture seems a little dry, add a few tablespoons of water.

Cook the pears, covered with a lid, for 10–15 minutes, or until they are broken down, fairly dry, and reduced.

Stir in the sugar and cook the chutney for another 5–10 minutes, or until thick and jam-like.

Serve as an accompaniment, either warm or at room temperature.

Lavash, also known as *nane lavash*, are ancient Persian breads popular in Iran. *Nane lavash* are so large they are impossible to bake in household ovens. Many versions of *lavash* breads are now becoming available in the West, especially the small crisp thin variety. If *lavash* (sometimes spelt *lawash*) are not easy to find, replace with split rounds of Lebanese breads, although the taste will not be the same.

Quick Pizza

Turkish breads, pide, make a soft and inviting pizza base. The recipe here has some of my favourite toppings — or try some of the varieties suggested below.

makes one 25cm (10-inch) pizza

Sauce

1½ tablespoons olive oil

½ teaspoon yellow asafetida powder

1½ cups tomato purée

1 tablespoon tomato paste

½ teaspoon each dried basil and oregano

1 teaspoon sugar

1 teaspoon salt

½ teaspoon freshly-ground black pepper

Topping

150g (5 ounces) fresh buffalo mozzarella, chopped coarsely

2 tablespoons grated Parmesan cheese

1 small eggplant, sliced into strips and fried

½ small red capsicum (pepper), diced

½ small green capsicum (pepper), diced

1/3 cup *kalamata* olives, pitted and halved

sprinkle dried oregano

one 25cm (10-inch) Turkish bread

The sauce: Heat the olive oil in a saucepan over moderate heat. Sprinkle in the yellow asafetida powder, sauté momentarily, add the rest of the ingredients and cook uncovered for 10–15 minutes or until fairly thick. Cool.

Assemble the pizza: Spread the sauce over the bread. Sprinkle with half the cheese, the remaining topping ingredients, and then the rest of the cheese.

Bake in a preheated 220°C/430°F oven for about 10 minutes or until the cheese is melted and bubbling.

Serve either warm or hot.

Some more pizza ideas

- Artichoke hearts, sundried tomatoes, *bocconcini*, rocket *pesto* and Parmesan.
- Pan-fried fresh fennel root with sundried tomatoes and fresh oregano.
- Tri-coloured grilled peppers with cherry tomatoes, olives and fresh *bocconcini*.
- Baby spinach, cottage cheese, semi-dried tomatoes, pine nuts and Parmesan.
- Potato with rosemary leaves.
- Asparagus with pine nut *pesto*, sundried capsicum and mozzarella.
- Sweet potato, oven-dried tomato halves, grilled baby eggplants, goat's cheese, olives and fresh oregano.
- Pizza *primavera*—tender broccoli florets, grilled zucchini and red peppers, asparagus, mozzarella, cheddar, roma tomatoes and Parmesan.

Bread Rolls with Bocconcini, Grilled
Eggplant, Sundried Capsicum & Basil

Snowy white, fresh bocconcini melted to unsurpassed succulence with juicy eggplant slices, fresh tomato sauce, sundried capsicum (peppers) and fragrant basil leaves, all wrapped in a soft bread roll. Sandwich heaven.

serves 4

4 soft white bread rolls

150g (5 ounces) sundried capsicum (pepper) in oil, sliced

one 200g (7-ounce) eggplant, sliced into large rings and pan-fried in olive oil until tender, or 1 cup marinated eggplant, drained

salt and pepper

300g (10 ounces) large balls fresh *bocconcini*, sliced into large thick rings

fresh tomato sauce (recipe follows)

20 large basil leaves

Preheat the griller.

Slice the buns in half. Top with slices of sundried capsicum, one ring of fried eggplant, a generous sprinkle of salt and freshly-ground black pepper, and a large ring of *bocconcini*.

Place under the griller until the cheese melts and spread with a generous spoon of fresh tomato sauce. Top with 5 large basil leaves.

Serve: Pop on the lid and serve immediately.

Fresh tomato sauce

1 teaspoon olive oil

¼ teaspoon yellow asafetida powder

2 large ripe tomatoes, blanched, peeled, seeded and finely chopped

a sprinkle each salt, pepper and sugar

1 teaspoon fresh basil leaves, chopped

Heat the olive oil in a small saucepan over moderate heat and briefly sauté the asafetida powder. Add the chopped tomato, salt, pepper, sugar and basil leaves.

Cook the sauce for 5–10 minutes, or until well reduced and pulpy. Remove from the heat, allow to cool then press through a sieve to form a smooth sauce. Discard the pulp, and use the sauce as directed above.

Fruit Delights

Although it was not originally intended as a breakfast food, Birchermuesli certainly fills that niche deliciously.

Birchermuesli

serves 4

²/₃ cup rolled oats (not instant) soaked in 1 cup of water overnight

juice of 1½ lemons

4 unwaxed apples

4 tablespoons each of freshly-ground almonds and hazelnuts

²/₃ cup yogurt

4 tablespoons honey

fresh seasonal fruits like peaches, apricots, bananas, melons or mango, sliced or chopped, to taste

fresh seasonal berries like raspberries, strawberries or blueberries, to taste

Place the soaked oats and whatever residual water remains with them in a large bowl along with the lemon juice.

Grate the unpeeled apples, and mix them into the oats and lemon to avoid discolouration.

Add the nuts, yogurt and honey and combine. Carefully fold in the sliced or chopped fruit.

Serve: Transfer to serving bowls and decorate with berries.

Note: The muesli will keep for 24 hours in the refrigerator. The apple might discolour, but this should not affect the taste.

Birchermuesli is named after its creator, Dr. Bircher Benner, who was ousted from the Swiss medical profession in 1900 for his heretical claims that grains, nuts, fruits and vegetables had more nutritional value than did meats. In formulating the muesli, Benner had in mind his many patients from wealthy families who were suffering the effects of a diet too high in protein.

Because Indonesia is hot all year round, various kinds of iced drinks called es are always popular, both day and night. The word teler in Jakarta slang, means 'intoxicated'. Of course this drink will not make you drunk, but the inference is that it will make you intoxicated with pleasure.

Indonesian Fruit Punch (Es Teler)

serves 4

100g (4 ounces) each of the following: ripe mango, avocado, papaya, pineapple, fresh or canned jackfruit, and red apple, all diced 1.5cm (½-inch)

1 immature coconut

1 teaspoon pure vanilla or *pandan* extract, or one fresh or frozen *pandan* leaf

300g (11 ounces) crushed ice

one 400g (14 ounce) can sweetened condensed milk, or two for a richer, sweeter punch

extra shaved ice for serving

Mix all the fruits in a large bowl.

Puncture the coconut, drain and collect all the water in a bowl. Completely open the coconut.

Scrape out teaspoon-sized lumps of the sweet immature coconut flesh with a melon baller, or a teaspoon. Combine with the coconut water.

Cut the fresh or frozen *pandan* leaf into 5cm (2-inch) lengths, place it in a large mortar, pour on ¼ cup boiling water and pound it with the pestle. Reserve the fragrant liquid and discard the leaf.

Combine the coconut water, coconut flesh, *pandan* or vanilla extract, or *pandan* water, ice and the sweetened condensed milk with the bowl of cut fruit. Mix well.

Serve: Ladle the mixture into large, tall chilled glasses, top each glass with shaved ice and serve with a spoon and a straw.

Note: Coconut water, not to be mistaken for coconut milk, is the clear juice from inside immature coconuts. It is available in the refrigerated cases of Asian supermarkets. For a thinner punch, add 2 cups of extra coconut water.

Select fresh, pink-fleshed guavas
at the peak of their season for this heavenly beverage.

Guava Thickshake

serves 4

300g (10 ounces) ripe, pink-fleshed
  guava (weigh after peeling—leave
  seeds in)
2 cups full-cream milk, chilled
2 tablespoons vanilla sugar
1/3 cup sweetened condensed milk
8 ice cubes

Pulse the guava flesh in a blender along
with the milk and vanilla sugar. Pour
through a fine strainer to separate out
the seeds.

Return the strained mixture to the
blender, process with the sweetened condensed milk and ice until frothy and thick.

Serve in chilled glasses.

Guava is the tropical fruit of the tree
Psidium guavaja. The acid-sweet fruit is
popular throughout Asia, where you will
often find it on street vendors' stalls. It is
unlikely that you have ever had a good guava
unless you live where they grow, for they are
best eaten within 24 hours of picking.
If you live near a Latin, West Indian or Indian
greengrocer who flies in fresh produce, look
for fruits that are scented. If the fruit is over-
ripe, the skin is usually greenish-yellow and
noticeably soft and smooth. Though the flesh
ranges in colour from creamy to pinkish-red,
most fruits contain tiny edible seeds in the
centre. Guavas are an excellent source of
vitamin C, containing 10 times the amount
found in oranges.

This smoothie is enriched with coconut milk. As an alternative, try milk, cream, buttermilk or yogurt.

Mango Coconut Smoothie

serves 4

flesh from 1 large ripe mango,
    about 400g (14 ounces)
1¾ cups coconut milk
1½ tablespoons fresh lime juice
    (from 1 large juicy lime)
2 tablespoons sugar
6 ice cubes

Process all the ingredients in a blender for 1 minute or until well combined. **Serve** immediately in chilled glasses.

The mango has held a special place in world cuisine for millennia. Eastern aficionados often refer to it as the 'king of fruits'. Its succulent, distinctively sweet-acid flesh is second to none. There are hundreds of varieties, several hundred species cultivated in India, for instance – and their flavours, colours and sizes vary enormously. Most supermarket mangoes are picked while still firm and pale green, but as they soften they develop orange-red, pink and yellow tones. The best eating mango is fibre-free, but even a stringy mango can be sweet and juicy.

Grilled Bananas with Yogurt, Maple Syrup & Toasted Macadamias

Grilled bananas always remind me of my childhood. When my father was occasionally inspired to cook, he would fry bananas in butter and sprinkle them with brown sugar as a quick dessert. This recipe expands the theme.

serves 6

6 firm ripe bananas
2 tablespoons butter, melted
¼ cup maple syrup or honey
¼ cup macadamias, toasted and chopped
sprinkle of ground cinnamon
1 cup Greek-style yogurt

Brush the bananas with the melted butter. Preheat the griller.
Grill, occasionally turning and brushing with more butter , until the bananas are soft and golden brown.
Serve: Drizzle the hot bananas with the maple syrup or honey, sprinkle with cinnamon and serve hot, accompanied with the Greek-style yogurt.

Warm Peaches with Roasted Almonds & Butter Lettuce

My recipe for this deliciously fruity salad is based on one by Julie Biuso from her book Take a Vine-ripened Tomato.   It also works well as an entrée.

serves 6

4 tablespoons light olive oil

²/₃ cup blanched almonds

sea salt flakes, such as Maldon salt

6 ripe but firm peaches

¾ teaspoon finely-ground
   coriander seeds

¼ teaspoon yellow
   asafetida powder

3 tablespoons lemon or lime juice

1½ teaspoons finely chopped
   tarragon

1 large butterleaf lettuce, washed
   and dried

freshly-ground black pepper

Heat 1 tablespoon of the oil in a small frying pan. When hot, stir in the almonds and toast them until lightly browned and fragrant. Transfer the almonds to a plate lined with paper towel, and drain them. While still warm, sprinkle the nuts with the salt.

Peel and slice the peaches and sprinkle with the coriander powder.

Warm the remaining olive oil in a wok or frying pan over moderate heat. Sprinkle in the yellow asafetida powder and fry momentarily. Toss in the peaches and warm them through for 1 minute. Pour in the lemon juice and sprinkle over the tarragon.

Serve: Arrange the lettuce leaves on a serving platter. Spoon the warm peaches and their juices over the lettuce. Scatter over the almonds, sprinkle with freshly-cracked black pepper and serve immediately.

Mangosteens, a native of Malaysia, are a round fruit with a thick, purple, leathery skin and a sweet, juicy and refreshing flesh. The creamy white flesh is divided into five, seven or nine segments, depending on the size of the fruit, which makes mangosteens very easy to eat.

Tropical Fruit Salad in Spicy Lemongrass

serves 6

1 ripe mango, peeled, segmented and
   cut into pieces
12 lychees, peeled and seeded
4 mangosteens, peeled and segmented
1 papaya, peeled, seeded and cut
   into pieces
200g (7 ounces) strawberries, trimmed
   and halved

Lemongrass Syrup

1¼ cups water
1¼ cups sugar
4 thin slices ginger
2 sticks lemongrass, white part only,
   bruised
1 tablespoon fresh lime juice

Mix the water, sugar, ginger and lemongrass in a saucepan and stir over medium heat to dissolve the sugar.

Simmer the syrup for 5 minutes for the flavours to combine.

Cool the syrup to room temperature, then strain. Add the lime juice and mix well.

Combine all the fruits in a large bowl, add the syrup and toss gently to mix.

Serve the fruit salad with scoops of ice cream.

Note: Mangosteens are now being grown in north Queensland, and can be found in the shops in March and April.

Mandarins originated in China, and are also known as tangerines.
In Australia, mandarins are available in the shops from March to November, but are at their best in the cooler months between May and August.

Fresh Citrus Selection in Mandarin Sauce with Crème Fraîche

serves 4

1 ruby grapefruit, peeled and cut in segments
1 yellow grapefruit, peeled and cut in segments
2 oranges, peeled and cut in segments
4 mandarins, peeled and separated into segments
1 cup *crème fraîche*

Mandarin Sauce

½ cup sugar
½ cup water
1 cinnamon stick, or a few pieces cassia bark
2 star anise
peel from half mandarin, cut in strips

Combine all the sauce ingredients in a saucepan and stir over medium heat until sugar dissolves. Bring to the boil and simmer for 5 minutes for the flavours to combine.
Cool the sauce to room temperature, then strain.
Mix all the fruits in a large bowl, add the syrup, and toss gently to combine.
Serve the citrus selection with dollops of *crème fraîche*.

Grapefruit Segments with Grenadine Syrup

Grenadine is a syrup made from the juice of the pomegranate. It is a bright red natural colouring agent with a sweet, fresh flavour. It looks particularly effective when added to sorbets, ice cream and fruit salads. Here it is simply drizzled over segments of freshly pared grapefruits.

serves 4

segments from 2 grapefruits
2 tablespoons grenadine syrup

Drizzle the syrup over the grapefruit segments.
Serve chilled.

Note: Don't mistake grenadine with pomegranate syrup (sometimes called pomegranate molasses), which is the unsweetened, boiled down juice of sour pomegranate seeds used especially in Middle Eastern cuisine.

Pears Platter
with Assorted Cheeses, Dried Fruits & Nuts

To my mind, pears and cheese are a match made in heaven. There are no rules or quantities for this recipe, just some suggested combinations. Serve as is, or with oat biscuits, walnut bread or crispy lavash bread.

Beurre Bosc Pears with Cheddar and Muscatel Raisins
Beurre Bosc pears are the ones with the lovely brown/cinnamon russet skin, thin tapering neck, curved stem and tender flesh. They're also great for baking and poaching. Purchase Beurre Bosc pears when they are firm but not hard. Allow them to ripen at room temperature, then store them in the fridge.

Packham Pears with Brie and Dried Figs
Soft, smooth, full-fat cow's milk cheese partners perfectly with the crisp, green-skinned juicy Packham pears.

Nashi Pears with Blue-vein Cheese and Walnuts
Also known as Asian pear, *Nashi* is the crisp fruit of the Japanese tree *Pyrus pyrofolia*. Its semi-sweet flesh and fragrant flavour is an excellent foil for the intense flavour and creaminess of blue-vein cheeses. Crisp walnuts round out the sensory experience.

This recipe was voted number one in our test kitchen
top 10 favourite desserts. It's incredibly easy, elegant and delicious.

Crisp Wonton Wrappers
with Fresh Berries & Cream

serves 6

12 square egg-free wonton
   wrappers
olive oil for shallow-frying
1 cup *crème fraîche*
1 cup thick cream
2 tablespoons sugar
300g (11 ounces) strawberries,
   hulled, halved and dredged in a
   little sugar, or berries of
   your choice
icing sugar for dusting

Shallow-fry the wonton wrappers a
few at a time in hot oil until golden
and puffed. Drain on absorbent
paper.

Combine the *crème fraîche*, thick
cream and sugar in a bowl and whisk
until soft peaks form.

Serve: Spoon the cream mixture
onto 6 wonton wrappers, top with
berries, cover each with another
wonton wrapper, and dust with
icing sugar.

Succulent stewed dried fruits couple wonderfully with the
ubiquitous Middle Eastern rice flour pudding known as muhallabeya.

Winter Fruit Compote with
Fragrant Syrian Milk Pudding

serves 6

300g (11 ounces) dried figs

1 cup sugar

1 vanilla bean, split

1 cinnamon stick

fine zest from 1 orange and ½ lemon

juice from 1 orange and half lemon

150g (5 ounces) pitted prunes

100g (4 ounces) dried apricots

200g (7 ounces) dried peaches

Soak the figs in hot water for 1 hour. Drain.

Combine the sugar, vanilla bean, cinnamon stick, zest and citrus juice in a saucepan, along with 1½ cups of water.

Bring to a boil, reduce the heat and simmer for 10 minutes. Add the dried figs along with the rest of the dried fruits, and simmer with a tightly fitting lid for ½ hour or until the fruits are tender. Cool to room temperature.

Serve with the fragrant milk pudding.

Fragrant Syrian Milk Pudding

Make sure you have a whisk on hand — there's some serious whiskin' ahead.

scant 1¼ cups rice flour

1.2 litres (2 pints) cold milk

½ cup sugar

1–2 tablespoons pure distilled rosewater

1–2 tablespoons chopped pistachio nuts

Every community has its own traditional flavourings and presentation for *muhallabeya*, some flavouring it with orange blossom water, or rosewater, and sprinkling it with chopped almonds or pistachios. The Turkish version uses vanilla or lemon zest, whereas the Iranians prefer cardamom.

Whisk the rice flour with a cup of the cold milk, adding it gradually and mixing thoroughly to avoid lumps.

Bring to the boil the rest of the milk in your heaviest pan.

Whisk in the rice flour and milk mixture, stirring vigorously. Cook on very low heat, stirring continuously for 10–15 minutes, or until the mixture thickens. Whisk in the sugar until dissolved then remove the saucepan from the heat and pour in the rosewater.

Whisk the whole mixture until creamy smooth, and chill.

Serve: Transfer the pudding to a large serving bowl, or individual ones, and sprinkle with the chopped pistachio nuts. Serve as an accompaniment to the fruit compote.

A fast, simple and exotic fruit dessert suggestion.

Char-grilled Mango & Pineapple Skewers
with Vanilla Ice Cream, Toasted Pecans & Hot Caramel Sauce

serves 6

2 large ripe mangoes, peeled,
   seeded and cut into 2cm
   (¾-inch) pieces
½ large ripe pineapple, cut into
   2cm (¾-inch) pieces

12 short bamboo skewers, soaked
   in water for 1 hour
2 tablespoons butter
50g (2 ounces) toasted pecan nuts
ice cream to serve
caramel sauce (recipe follows)

Thread the mango and pineapple pieces alternately onto the skewers.
Place in a shallow oven-proof glass or ceramic dish, and drizzle with butter.
Grill until browned on the edges.
Serve with scoops of vanilla ice cream topped with chopped toasted pecans and drizzled with hot caramel sauce.

Hot Caramel Sauce

2 tablespoons butter
1 cup dark brown sugar
½ cup water
1 tablespoon cornflour
   (cornstarch)
1 teaspoon pure vanilla extract
½ cup cream

Combine the butter and sugar in a saucepan over moderate heat, and stir constantly until the butter melts.
Whisk together the water, cornflour (cornstarch), vanilla and cream, and add to the saucepan.
Simmer the sauce over low heat until the sugar dissolves. Bring the sauce to the boil, then reduce the heat and simmer for three minutes.
Serve hot. Makes 1½ cups.

Indian Fruit Platter (Phal Chat)

A simple dessert in Australia might be fruit and cream, and in France it might be fruit and cheese. In India it would be several types of fruits cut in their prime of ripeness, served plain or with a sprinkle of lime juice, salt, pepper, black salt or a spice blend called chat masala. Fruit combinations are endless; here are some suggested combinations.

Fruit Combinations

- mandarins (tangerines), blueberries and cherimoyas (custard apple)
- oranges and papaya slices with pineapple cubes
- avocado, grapefruit segments and stuffed fresh dates
- sweet cherries, bananas and yellow peaches
- sliced pears, seeded green grapes and prickly pears
- guava cubes, kiwi slices and persimmons
- apple slices, raspberries and fresh figs
- cucumber slices, strawberries and blue plum wedges
- passionfruit, lychees and cape gooseberries
- carambolas (star fruits), tangelos and pomegranates
- mixed melon platter

Crème Fraîche & Cardamom Dressing

1 cup *crème fraîche*, yogurt or sour cream
2 tablespoons honey
2 tablespoons orange juice
1 teaspoon ground cardamom

Other suggested accompaniments

wedges of limes or lemons
sprinkle of salt, pepper or black salt
sprinkle of *chat masala*

Fruit Juice Dressing

1/3 cup lime juice
1/3 cup orange juice
3 tablespoons honey
2 tablespoons olive oil
2 tablespoons finely-chopped mint

Combine any of the above fruit combinations with either of the suggested dressings or accompaniments.

Note: Try threading the fruit on bamboo skewers. Also note that some fruits require dipping in lemon or lime juice to prevent discolouration. Black salt and *chat masala* are available at Indian grocers.

Fools are the most popular surviving members of a venerable English family of desserts that also include flummeries, trifles and syllabubs. Recipes for these delicious, rich fruit creams have held their own in British cookbooks since the 17th century.

Custard Apple Fool

serves 4

2 cups custard apple pulp
juice of 2 limes, strained
2 cups lightly whipped cream

Pass the fruit pulp through a sieve and mix the sieved pulp with the lime juice and lightly whipped cream.

Serve: Pour into tall dessert glasses and serve immediately.

Traditional English fools include raspberries, gooseberries, rhubarb or blackberries. This recipe is a new fool on the block that takes advantage of the delectablevirtues of custard apples (cherimoya). For other new-age fools, try kiwi fruit, blueberries or mango.

Brazilian Chayote and Orange Appetiser (Salada de Xuxu)

The pear-shaped, green-skinned vegetable with the large white pip known as chayote in Latin America and the Caribbean is none other than the Aussie choko. The vegetable has a rather bland, neutral flavour with a fresh juicy texture, and it combines well with other vegetables and fruits, especially with citrus flavours, as in this refreshingly different appetizer-cum-salad.

serves 4

2 chokos, peeled, seeded and
   shredded
3 oranges, peeled and cut into thin
   segments, juice reserved
heart of one iceberg lettuce, sliced
   thin (*chiffonade*)
1 hot green chili, seeded and julienned
1 tablespoon extra-virgin olive oil
juice from 2 limes
¼ teaspoon yellow asafetida powder
1 teaspoon salt
½–¾ teaspoon freshly-ground black
   pepper
3 sprigs fresh coriander, mint or
   parsley, finely chopped
more chopped herbs for garnish

Combine the chokos, orange, lettuce and chili in a serving bowl.
Whisk together the oil, lime juice, asafetida, salt and pepper in a small bowl.
Pour the dressing over the fruit and vegetables. Fold in the chopped herbs and toss to combine. Refrigerate then toss again.
Serve with a garnish of the fresh herbs.

Note: *Chayote* is a Spanish name, but in Brazil, where Portuguese is spoken, it is known as *xuxu* (pronounced *'shoe-shoe'*). Select glossy, dark green chokos the colour of Granny Smith apples; they are the freshest.

Desserts & Sweets

Apple Strudel

The quickest way to make strudel these days is with bought puff pastry or filo pastry. We tested strudel made from both, and the results were so good we couldn't make up our mind which one was better. Here's the filo variety.

serves 8–10

20 sheets of filo pastry (thick
  variety is best)
175g (6 ounces) melted
  unsalted butter
icing sugar to sprinkle

Filling

1kg (2 pounds) tart green apples
juice of 1 lemon
4 tablespoons sugar
100g (4 oz) walnuts, coarsely
  chopped
1 cup golden raisins
1 teaspoon cinnamon powder
75g (3 oz) ground almonds, or dry
  fine breadcrumbs

Preheat the oven to 180°C/350°F.

Peel, core and finely chop or dice the apples. Immediately mix with the lemon juice to avoid discolouration. Mix in the rest of the filling ingredients.

Divide the filling into four. Open the packet of filo pastry just before using. Unroll the sheets and leave them in a pile.

Brush the top one lightly with melted butter and put it to one side. Brush 4 more with melted butter and put them on top. Put one quarter of the filling in a line along one long edge, about 6cm (2½ inches) from the edge and 2cm (¾-inch) from the sides.

Lift the edge up over the filling and roll up, not too tightly, tucking in the sides half-way so the filling does not fall out. Lift the roll and carefully place on a buttered baking dish or tray, seam-side down. Brush the surface with butter. Repeat for the other 3 *strudel* rolls.

Bake for 30–40 minutes or until golden brown and crispy. Remove from the oven, cool slightly, and dust with icing sugar.

Serve the *strudel* warm or at room temperature, cut into slices.

Apple *strudel* is popular all over Eastern Europe, and traditionally uses a wafer-thin pastry that is painstakingly made from scratch. Apparently this pastry originated in the Middle East and was brought to Europe in the Ottoman invasions of the 15th century.

This simple and sublime dessert is popular, in one form or another, all over South-East Asia. In Thailand, where it is known as khaoneow mamuang it is eaten not just as a dessert, but as a sweet afternoon snack, or any time.

Thai Sticky Rice with Mango

serves 4

2 cups sticky (glutinous) white rice, soaked in cold water for 1 hour, then drained

1¼ cups coconut milk, one 400ml can

pinch salt

2 tablespoons sugar

2 large ripe mangoes

2 tablespoons coconut milk to serve

mint leaves to decorate

Combine the rice, coconut milk, salt and sugar in an uncovered saucepan with 1¼ cups of water. Stir and bring to the boil over moderate heat. **Simmer** the rice, stirring, for about 8-10 minutes, or until all the liquid has been absorbed. Remove from the heat, cover the pan, and leave it to stand for 5 minutes.

Transfer the rice to a steamer or double saucepan, and steam it for 15–20 minutes.

Spoon the hot steamed sticky rice into 6-8 individual ramekins or indi-vidual pudding moulds lined with plastic wrap and set them aside to cool.

Serve: Remove the rice from the mould, and place one portion in the centre of each dessert plate. Arrange the mango around it, and drizzle the rice with the reserved coconut milk. Garnish with mint leaves.

Note: as an alternative serving sug-gestion, press the warm rice evenly into a tray lined with plastic wrap. When cold cut into diamond-shaped pieces.

Sticky rice can be served with a variety of fruits—typically mango, jackfruit or durian. It is also some-times eaten with palm sugar syrup, with thick coconut milk and a pinch of salt, sprinkled with sesame, or served with a type of coconut milk custard called *sankhaya*. You can even serve it with sweetened or un-sweetened cream.

Individual Rhubarb Crumbles

Baked desserts look especially attractive when presented in individual ramekins. These little rhubarb crumbles are no exception.

serves 8

1kg (2 pounds) rhubarb stems, washed, trimmed and cut into small pieces

½ cup sugar

2 tablespoons softened butter for ramekin dishes

Crumble Topping

1 teaspoon ginger powder

1 teaspoon baking powder

1½ cups plain flour

¾ cup raw sugar

¼ cup unsalted butter, softened

thick cream to serve

Place the rhubarb and ½ cup sugar in a covered saucepan.

Simmer over moderate heat with whatever water clings to the fruit for about 10 minutes, or until the rhubarb is tender.

Preheat the oven to 190°C/375°F.

Brush 8 ramekin dishes (1-cup capacity) with the softened butter. Divide the rhubarb mixture evenly between the prepared dishes to 2cm (¾-inch) from the top.

Prepare the topping: Place the ginger, baking powder, flour and raw sugar into a mixing bowl. Stir to combine. Rub in the softened butter with your fingers until the mixture resembles coarse breadcrumbs.

Spread the topping evenly over each dessert, filling each ramekin to the top. Place the ramekins into a baking tray.

Bake in the preheated oven for 15–20 minutes, or until the juice from the fruit starts to bubble through the crumble topping. Remove from the oven.

Serve each crumble immediately with a spoonful of thick cream.

Also known as kuih buah melaka, these delicious dumplings derive their pleasantly chewy texture from glutinous rice flour. All the ingredients for onde-onde are available at Asian supermarkets.

Indonesian Sticky Coconut Dumplings (Onde-Onde)

makes 20 dumplings

one 20cm (8-inch) strip of fresh or frozen *pandan* leaf

few drops green colouring

1¼ cups glutinous (sticky) rice flour

¼ cup plus 1½ tablespoons boiling water

60g (2 ounces) palm sugar cut into small pieces

1 cup freshly-grated coconut mixed with a pinch salt

Pound and squeeze the *pandan* leaf in a mortar and pestle with 2 tablespoons of hot water to extract its fragrant juice.

Sift the glutinous rice flour into a bowl.

Pour in a combination of the boiling water and 1 tablespoon of the *pandan* juice mixed with the green food colouring. Mix well and knead into a firm lump of dough.

Roll the mixture into marble-size balls. Flatten each ball slightly and insert 1 or 2 pieces of palm sugar. Fully enclose the sugar, and re-shape into balls, making sure that the dough is fully sealed with no cracks or exposed sugar. If cracks appear, simply moisten them with water and seal again.

Bring water to the boil in a large saucepan, and drop in half the balls. When cooked, the balls will rise to the surface. Remove them with a slotted spoon, shake them dry and immediately roll them in the grated coconut.

Serve warm or cold.

The *pandan* leaf (sometimes referred to as screwpine) is an aromatic member of the *pandanus* family. After tying each leaf in a knot, they are often added to Indonesian, Malay and Nyonya rice and sweet dishes, while the juice is extracted for sweetmeats known in Malaysia as *kuis*, of which the above are a famous example.

Aussie Anzac Cookies

Famous Aussie cookies that are quick to bake.

makes 24

1 cup rolled oats
1 cup plain flour
1 cup sugar
¾ cup coconut
½ cup butter
1 tablespoon golden syrup
   or treacle
1 teaspoon baking soda
2 tablespoons water

Preheat the oven to 150°C/300°F. Combine the oats, flour, sugar and coconut in a bowl and mix well.

Melt the butter and syrup together in a small saucepan.

Boil the water in another small saucepan. Sprinkle the soda into the boiling water and add this to the melted butter and syrup. It will froth up. Add this foamy mixture to the dry ingredients and mix well.

Place tablespoonfuls of the mixture on 2 large buttered trays.

Bake in the upper half of the oven for 20 minutes, or until the cookies are golden. Allow the cookies to cool a little on the trays before removing.

Serve when cool.

Note: For a slightly different textured Anzac that melts in the oven to a crisper consistency, use 2 tablespoons golden syrup and 3 tablespoons boiling water.

These muffins are completely dairy-free and almost totally fat-free. They are also egg-free, but certainly not taste-free, and their moist texture has to be experienced to be believed. They're based on a recipe from the renowned The Golden Door Health Retreat in Australia's sunshine state, Queensland.

Maple Fruit Muffins

makes 12 muffins

1 cup pitted semi-dried California dates, chopped

½ cup maple syrup or mild honey

1 teaspoon bicarbonate of soda

grated rind and juice of 2 oranges

3 green apples, peeled and grated

3 cups wholemeal self-raising flour

1 teaspoon ground cinnamon

1 cup sultanas

½ cup walnuts, chopped

cottage cheese blended with honey and cinnamon to serve

Preheat the oven to 180°C/350°F.

Combine the dates, maple syrup or honey, bicarbonate of soda and 1 cup water in a saucepan, bring to the boil and simmer over low heat for 2 minutes. Cool to room temperature.

Fold together the remaining ingredients, and stir in the date mixture. Mix well and spoon into 12 non-stick muffin tins.

Bake for 25–30 minutes, or until the muffins are golden and fully cooked.

Serve the muffins warm or at room temperature for a snack, or with the sweetened cottage cheese for dessert.

Pears Croustada

Pears croustada is an extremely delicious combination of flaky puff pastry, marzipan and cream cheese that's baked in the oven with sliced almonds until puffed and golden and served warm with whipped cream. Are you salivating yet? If so, proceed on.

makes 8 pastries

8 squares 12cm (4½ inch) raw
  puff pastry
400g (14 ounces) cream cheese, cut
  into small pieces
200g (7 ounces) marzipan, cut into
  small pieces
2 tablespoons sugar
3 ripe firm pears, peeled, cored and
  thinly sliced
little extra sugar for sprinkling
50g (2 ounces) flaked almonds
whipped cream for serving

Preheat the oven to 200°C/400°F.
Place the puff pastry squares on two baking sheets lined with baking paper.
Combine the cream cheese, marzipan and sugar. Scatter the mixture over the pastry squares. Arrange the pears over the marzipan mixture, and sprinkle with a little more sugar and the flaked almonds.
Bake for 15–20 minutes, or until the pastry is puffed and golden.
Serve warm with whipped cream.
Note: As an excellent alternative to pears, try Golden Delicious apples, an excellent cooking apple that holds its shape well.

This irresistible dessert can be served in two ways. You can smother the freshly cooked crisp hot doughnuts with the cold, smooth, fruit-studded yogurt for an experience of contrasting textures and temperatures. Alternatively, if you leave the doughnuts in the yogurt, they swell up and become succulent, soft and spongy, drinking up the juices and flavours of their sauce. The choice is yours.

Anise-flavoured Doughnuts in Mango Yogurt (Malpoura)

serves 6–8

2¼ cups self-raising flour

1 tablespoon freshly-ground fennel seeds

¼ cup fine sugar

approximately 1¼ cups cold water

1 teaspoon yogurt

ghee or oil for deep-frying

Yogurt Sauce

4 cups plain yogurt

¾ cup sugar

2 large mangoes cut into chunks

For the doughnuts: Mix together the flour, fennel and sugar in a bowl. Gradually whisk in the water and teaspoon of yogurt until the mixture becomes a fairly thick batter. Allow the batter to rest for 10 minutes.

For the sauce: Whisk the yogurt and sugar together and fold in the mango pieces. Set aside.

Heat ghee or oil in a wok or deep pan over moderate heat. When fairly hot—about 160°C/320°F—spoon out tablespoonfuls of batter, and with the aid of a second spoon, scoop the batter into the hot oil.

Fry as many cakes as can be comfortably fried at one time. Remember they swell as they fry. Turn and cook them evenly, for 2–3 minutes on each side, or until light golden brown.

Remove and drain on paper towels. Continue frying until all the batter is used up.

Serve the doughnuts hot, smothered with the mango yogurt, or leave them to plump up and soak.

Note: Try these alternative flavours: fresh berries of your choice, banana, passionfruit, kiwifruit or papaya.

Quick Cherry Cheesecake

This delectable and good-looking cheesecake requires no baking.

It features a biscuit crumb base and a filling of cream cheese folded with plump sour cherries.

makes one 20cm (8-inch)
  cheesecake

180g (6 ounces) fairly plain sweet
  biscuits

100g (4 ounces) butter, chopped

1 teaspoon bitter almond extract

one 400g (14-ounce) tin
  sweetened condensed milk

½ cup freshly squeezed lemon juice

1 teaspoon pure vanilla extract

250g (9 ounces) cream cheese,
  chopped

1 tablespoon cornflour
  (cornstarch)

1¼ cups sour cherries in syrup,
  drained well

¼ cup sour cherries, plus ½ cup
  syrup reserved for topping

Prepare the base: Process the biscuits in a food processor until a fine powder. Drop in the butter and the bitter almond extract. Process until the mixture is fully blended. Remove the mixture and press it evenly into the base and up the sides of a pre-buttered 20cm (8-inch) fluted pie tin.

Prepare the filling: Add the condensed milk, lemon juice, vanilla and cream cheese to the food processor and blend until smooth. Remove the mix to a bowl. Fold in the 1¼ cups drained sour cherries. Pour the mixture into the prepared crust.

Prepare the topping: Combine the cornflour (cornstarch) with a couple of teaspoons cherry syrup to make a runny paste. Combine with the remaining syrup and the reserved sour cherries in a small saucepan, and stirring, bring the mixture to a boil over moderate heat. When the mixture thickens, quickly pour it over the top of the cheesecake and spread it as desired.

Chill the cheesecake for at least 3 hours before removing from its base.

Serve: The cheesecake is at its best served the next day.

Note: For a quicker setting time, place the cheesecake (before you add the cherry topping) in a pre-warmed 175°C/345°F oven for 10 minutes. Remove, top with the cherry topping, and chill for 2 hours.

makes 24 biscuits

175g (6 ounces) butter

½ cup caster sugar

2½ cups plain flour

1 teaspoon ground cardamom
   seeds

icing sugar for sprinkling

Preheat the oven to 160°C/325°F.
Cream the butter with the caster
sugar in a food processor. Add the
flour and cardamom, and process to
form a soft dough.

Roll the mixture into 24 walnut-
sized balls. Arrange them on baking
sheets lined with baking paper about
2cm (¾-inch) apart. Press them
gently with the flat underside of fork
tines to slightly flatten and mark
them with decorative lines.

Bake for about 25 minutes. The
biscuits will hardly darken, and will
appear undercooked, but they will
firm up when they cool.

Serve: Remove from the paper
only when they have hardened, and
dredge them in icing sugar.

Cardamom-scented
Butter Biscuits (Shakar Lemah)

Anyone who enjoys a good shortbread will love these melt-in-the-mouth delights
from Iraq. They are exceptionally easy to make.

Semolina Syrup Cake (Basbousa)

The Middle East has a long tradition of delicious sweets. Whereas some are time consuming, this delectable Eguptian recipe is a breeze to prepare, and is especially suited to cooking in big quantities. In some ways basbousa reminds me of Indian halava, but it's easier to make. Basbousa is at the peak of perfection if it's left to soak overnight.

serves 10 or more

2 cups fine semolina
1 cup dried coconut threads
½ cup sugar
150g (5 ounces) butter, melted
1 cup milk

Syrup
1½ cups sugar
1½ cups water
2 tablespoons fresh lemon juice

Preheat the oven to 175°C/345°F.

Whisk together the semolina, coconut and sugar in a bowl. Add the butter and milk. Mix until well combined.

Pour the mixture into a buttered, shallow, medium-sized dish.

Bake for 30 minutes, or until lightly golden brown.

Prepare the syrup: Slowly dissolve the sugar in the water in a medium-sized saucepan over low heat. Increase the heat to moderate and boil the syrup until it reduces by about one-third, or until it just coats the back of a spoon. Add the lemon juice.

Cut the completed cake into diamond shapes while it's still hot, and pour the hot syrup over. It will seem like a lot of syrup, but it will all gradually soak in.

Serve at room temperature. Best served the next day.

Batter-fried Bananas (Pisang Goreng)

In the tropics, many varieties of bananas are suitable for pisang goreng, each with its own distinctive flavour. Ordinary bananas are perfectly good, but even better are ripe yellow plantains, which fry with a firmer texture. Whichever variety of banana you choose, this dessert of Malaysian and Indonesian fame will always be popular, especially served with ice cream and drizzled with maple or palm sugar syrup.

serves 4–6

½ cup rice flour
¼ cup cornflour (cornstarch)
¼ cup plain flour
¼ teaspoon baking powder
½ teaspoon salt
2 tablespoons oil
1 cup coconut milk
8 fairly ripe bananas
oil or ghee for deep frying
ice cream and maple syrup to serve

Sift the rice flour, corn flour, plain flour, baking powder and salt into a bowl.

Mix the oil with the coconut milk. Gradually stir into the dry ingredients until the mixture forms a fairly thick, smooth batter. Adjust the consistency with a little water if necessary.

Cut the bananas crossways into 3 pieces, or into sizes of your choice.

Heat the ghee or oil in a deep pan. When the oil is fairly hot, dip a few pieces of banana in the batter and coat well.

Deep-fry them in the hot oil, turning when required, for about 3–4 minutes per batch, or until evenly golden brown.

Remove the fritters from the oil with a slotted spoon and drain on kitchen paper. Keep them warm while frying the remaining batches.

Serve hot, warm or cold.

Little Berry Puddings

These dainty little desserts are great to bake with small, peak-of-the-season fresh berries. Blackberries work particularly well, as do raspberries. Try them with small loganberries, boysenberries or youngberries.

makes 6 puddings

60g (2 ounces) butter
¼ cup fine sugar
¼ cup light sour cream
1 teaspoon vanilla extract
125g (4 ounces) self-raising flour
enough cold milk for a dropping
　consistency batter (up to 1 cup)
2 punnets small berries of
　your choice

Preheat the oven to 180°C/350°F. Liberally butter 6 dariole moulds or individual custard cups.

Cream the butter and sugar together until light and fluffy. Beat in the sour cream and vanilla. Fold the flour into the mixture, a little at a time, adding sufficient milk to form a dropping consistency.

Cover the base of each mould with a layer of berries. Divide the pudding batter evenly between each of the moulds. Cover the top of each with aluminium foil, sealing tightly at the edges.

Place the moulds in a baking dish along with sufficient hot water to come two-thirds of the way up the sides of the moulds.

Bake on the centre shelf of the oven for about 30 minutes, or until the mixture has risen and is spongy to the touch.

Run a small knife around each pudding, then carefully turn out onto individual serving dishes.

Serve at once with cream and extra berries on the side.

Popular throughout Italy, especially in the south and Sicily, croccante (literally 'crunchy') is a mixture of caramelised sugar and almonds that are left to harden. It is then broken into pieces for use as a confection or ground up for use as a flavouring. Croccante is fairly simple to prepare, but it must be handled quickly and deftly to avoid the sugar overcooking and becoming bitter, as well as to avoid burns.

Sicilian Almond Brittle (Croccante)

makes 2 cups

1 cup sugar

1 tablespoon light corn syrup

1½ cups whole, blanched almonds, lightly toasted

Combine the sugar and corn syrup in a wide, heavy pan over low heat. Stir continuously with a metal spoon until the mixture looks like wet sand. Allow the mixture to melt and caramelise, stirring occasionally. Meanwhile, have a clean heatproof platter nearby on which to spread the finished brittle.

Remove the pan from the heat when the sugar is a clear, amber colour.

Stir in the almonds quickly, and pour the molten *croccante* out of the pan onto the waiting platter. Very quickly spread it out with the spoon. Allow the *croccante* to cool and harden.

Serve: Break the *croccante* into pieces, or use as required.

Buttermilk Scones with Jam & Cream

The best scones I ever ate were in Devon on a holiday as a boy with my family. I can still clearly picture the little teahouse, and the warm scones, buttered and slathered with clotted cream so thick that it stood up on its own, a dollop of strawberry jam at its peak.

makes 12 scones

1¾ cups plain flour

1 teaspoon sugar

1 teaspoon salt

2 teaspoons baking powder

½ teaspoon baking soda

5 tablespoons room temperature
 unsalted butter

¾ cup buttermilk, approximately

butter, jam and cream to serve

Making good scones is not difficult, and they get easier with practise. The two golden rules of scone making are these: Add the wet ingredients to the dry, and mix the dough as briefly and lightly as possible. And remember, the lighter the touch, the lighter the scones.

The lightest scones are those made with buttermilk, although you can also use milk or soured milk.

Scones made with cream are the richest, with a very smooth taste and texture.

The traditional scone can also be varied with the addition of raisins. Scones should be eaten within a few hours, but they can be frozen in a bag for up to three months.

Preheat the oven to 230°C/450°F. Brush a baking tray with butter.

Sift all the dry ingredients together in a bowl (sifting aerates the mix). Rub the butter into the dry mix briefly and lightly, using your fingertips, until fine and crumbly.

Make a well in the centre of the dry ingredients, and add almost all the buttermilk.

Mix, using a knife in a quick cutting motion while rotating the bowl. The mixture will come together in small pieces. Mix in the rest of the buttermilk if the mix is too dry.

Gather the dough together, and turn it out onto a clean, lightly floured surface.

Knead the dough very lightly, folding it back over itself, pressing down, and turning, for 30–40 seconds. The dough should have just lost its stickiness.

Roll or press the dough out to a flat round about 1.5cm (½-inch) thick. Cut out rounds of about 4cm (1½ inches). Pile the scraps together and press or roll out, but don't re-knead them.

Use up all the dough. Place the scones on the tray

Bake the scones for 10–12 minutes, or until well-risen and golden on top. Remove from the oven. For soft scones, wrap them while warm in a clean tea towel. For scones with a crisp top, transfer to a wire rack to cool slightly.

Serve with butter, jam and cream.

Little Saffron, Lemon
& Coconut cakes

Saffron is one of my favourite kitchen ingredients. Its warm, heady fragrance and brilliant colour marries wonderfully with the citrus hit of lemon zest. Coupled with coconut, the trio does a great job in flavouring and colouring these little cakes.

makes 12 little cakes

½ teaspoon saffron thread, ground and infused in 2 teaspoons of the milk

1 ¾ cups self-raising flour

½ teaspoon baking powder

½ cup butter

½ cup caster sugar

1 tablespoon fine lemon zest

4 tablespoons sour light cream

½ cup dessicated coconut

1 ¼ cups milk

Topping

2 cups icing sugar

2 tablespoons soft butter

2 tablespoons lemon juice

¼ teaspoon reserved saffron infusio

Reserve ¼ teaspoon of the saffron infusion for the topping.

Preheat the oven to 160°C/325°F. Sift together the flour and baking powder.

Cream the butter, sugar and lemon zest together in a large bowl until light and fluffy. Stir in the sour cream and the saffron infusion, and beat to fully blend.

Stir in the coconut, half the milk, and sift in half the flour. Mix well. Fold in the remaining flour and the milk. Mix until evenly blended.

Spoon the mixture into pre-buttered small cupcake or muffin tins.

Bake for 20 minutes, or until golden brown, well risen and spongy. Turn off the heat, but allow the cakes to stand in the closed oven for an extra 5 minutes before removing and cooling on wire racks.

Prepare the topping: Sift the icing sugar into a bowl. Stir in the butter and the reserved saffron infusion. Heat the lemon juice in a small saucepan until almost boiling. Pour sufficient lemon juice into the icing sugar mixture to form a firm paste. Ice the cakes while the topping is still warm.

Serve warm or cool.

> **Note for European and American readers:** To make your own self-raising flour, combine 1 cup/4oz/100g soft, all purpose, plain flour with 1 teaspoon baking powder and ⅛ teaspoon bicarbonate of soda.

Glossary

Abura-age-dofu
Deep-fried tofu slices that are stuffed with flavoured *sushi* rice to prepare the well-known sweet-savoury Japanese finger food *inari-zushi*. Since it is not possible to prepare *abura-age-dofu* at home, you will need to obtain them from well-stocked Asian grocers, where they come either in shrink-wrapped pouches or in cans.

Acidulate
To add an acid (e.g. lemon juice or vinegar) to a liquide or mixture to prevent browning of fruits or vegetables.

Achiote
(see *annato*)

Annato
The evergreen flowering tree, *Bixa orellana* have heart-shaped scarlet fruits that yield rust-red seeds, which when fried, yield a bright orange-yellow colour. Also known as *achiote*, this natural colouring agent is used in Caribbean and Philippine dishes. *Annato* seeds are available at Latin and some Asian grocers.

Arborio Rice
A short, highly glutinous fat-grained rice variety grown in Italy and classified as *superfino*. It is used in the preparation of *risotto*. *Arborio* rice is available at well-stocked super-markets.

Asafetida
The aromatic resin from the root of the giant fennel, *Ferula asafoetida*. Also known as *hing*, it is extracted from the stems of these giant perennials that grow wild in Central Asia. Due to the presence of sulphur compounds, raw asafetida has a distinctive pungent aroma. To cook asafetida, small amounts are fried in a little oil before adding to a variety of savoury dishes,

adding a pleasant flavour reminiscent of a mixture of garlic and shallots. I always use the mild yellow asafetida powder, available at Indian and Asian grocers and well-stocked specialty stores.

Badis
Sundried legume nuggets that can be reconstituted in vegetable stews, pasta sauces and Mexican dishes. Also known as *warian* and *wadi*, they are available at well-stocked Indian grocers.

Balsamic Vinegar
A highly fragrant, sweetish vinegar from Italy made from concentrated grape juice and aged in wood for at least 10 years.

Banh Trang
Vietnamese rounds of thin, whitish rice-paper sheets that are dipped in water to become flexible wrappers for a variety of spring rolls. The sealed packets, available at Asian grocers, will last indefinitely in their dried state, although they are brittle and can break easily if dropped.

Bangkwang
(see yam bean)

Basil
The fragrant aromatic herb *Ocimum basilicum*, known also as sweet basil. It is a small, profusely branched bushy plant whose tender green leaves are used worldwide, especially in Italian cuisine. There are many types of basil, which vary in size, flavour and colour, and all can be used for culinary purposes.

Basmati Rice
A superb, light-textured, long grained rice from North India and Pakistan, with a wonderful fragrance and flavour. Available at Asian and Indian grocers and well-stocked supermarkets.

Bay Leaves
The leaves of the sweet bay or laurel tree, *Laurus nobilis*, an evergreen member

of the laurel family native to the Mediterranean region and Asia Minor. The highly aromatic leaves are thick, dark green and glossy on their upper surface. They can be used fresh or dried, and are quite pungent with a slightly bitter, spicy flavour.

Bean Curd
(see tofu)

Besan Flour
(see chickpea flour)

Black Beans, Chinese
Fermented and salted black soya beans that are available in jars or plastic bags from Asian grocers. They are ready to use straight from the packet, needing only a brief rinse in water before use.

Black Pepper
(see pepper)

Black Salt
A reddish-grey variety of salt with a distinct hard-boiled egg flavour. Known in India as *kala namak*, it is a major ingredient in the spice blend known as *chat masala*. It is available at Indian grocers.

Bocconcini
A fresh, Italian mild-flavoured cheese, a little like mozzarella. It is hand-moulded into creamy white balls and sold swimming in whey. Ideally, it should be eaten as soon as possible after buying. If unavailable, fresh Italian mozzarella made from the milk of water buffaloes (*mozzarella di buffala*) is an excellent alternative.

Bok Choy
The common Cantonese name for Chinese cabbage. These small cabbages used in Chinese cooking have dark green leaves and wide white stalks. The smaller the individual cabbage, the more delicate the flavour. *Bok choy* is available at Chinese grocers.

Buttermilk

Real buttermilk is the liquid residue after cream has been churned into butter. However, the buttermilk referred to in this book is cultured buttermilk, a low fat milk that has been cultured in a similar way to yogurt to produce a mild-tasting dairy product with a consistency like light cream. Available at most well-stocked supermarkets.

Caraway

Caraway seeds are the fruits of the hardy biennial herb *Carum carvi*, a native of Europe, Asia and North Africa. The brown seeds are curved and tapered at one end, and are sometimes mistaken for cumin seeds, although they taste quite different. Caraway seeds are warm, sweet, biting and pleasantly acrid. They are a favourite flavouring for many kinds of rye bread and are also used in cheese, cakes and biscuits.

Cardamom

The world's third most costly spice, topped only by vanilla and saffron. The odour and flavour of cardamom seeds is reminiscent of lemon zest and eucalyptus. Cardamom is used in Indian and Middle Eastern cooking, especially rice dishes and sweets. Best purchased as whole pods from Indian or Middle Eastern grocers.

Carob

The edible beans from the carob tree, a legume belonging to the locust family. The beans grown on this tall evergreen tree are dried, ground to a powder and used as one would use cocoa. Carob is also rich in protein. Available at specialty and health stores.

Capers

The pickled flower bud of the wild Mediterranean bush *Capparis rupestris*. Capers have been used as a condiment for thousands of years, and they feature especially in French and Italian cuisine. They have a distinct sour, salty flavour and are available at all Mediterranean grocers.

Cayenne Pepper

The orange-red to deep-red powder derived from small sundried pungent red chili peppers. This bitingly hot condiment should be used with restraint, for a small amount will add considerable zest and flavour to dishes, notably in Indian and Mexican cuisine. Cayenne is available from supermarkets or well-stocked grocers.

Chat Masala

A traditional companion to cut fruit in Indian cuisine. This light-brown spice blend contains a number of ingredients, notably black salt, mango powder and asafetida. *Chat masala* is available from Indian grocers.

Chayote

A fairly bland, green pear-shaped squash similar in size to the avocado, which grows on the rampant vine *Sechium edule*. Originally from South America, it is now grown in Australia, the Caribbean and the US, Commonly known outside of South America as *choko*.

Chickpeas

Also called *garbanzo* beans and *ceci* beans. The hard, dried round peas are about ⅓ inch in diameter and biscuit to light brown in colour with a wrinkled surface. The flavour is nut-like and the texture firm. Chickpeas are available dried, bottled and canned. Raw chickpeas should be soaked for 8 hours before cooking. Remember to discard the soaking water before boiling in fresh water.

Chickpea Flour

The finely milled, pale yellow flour from ground, roasted *chana dal*. It is popular in Indian cuisine for making batter, as a binding agent, and in confectionery. It is also known as *besan* flour and *gram* flour. Chickpea flour is available at Indian grocers.

Chiffonade

A garnish or base for other foods made from a very finely sliced roll of lettuce, sorrel or other green leaves.

Chipotle

A smoked, dried red *jalapeño* chili, usually dark brown to coffee colour with cream veins and ridges. It has a distinctive smoky hot flavour.

Chilies

(see individual entries)

Choko

(see *chayote*)

Choy Sum

A delicately flavoured vegetable with yellow flowers and succulent green stalks, used extensively in Chinese and Japanese cuisine. Available from Chinese greengrocers all year round.

Ciabatta

A firm, flat and crusty oval-shaped Italian bread.

Cinnamon

Thin sundried sheaths of bark from the moderate-sized bushy evergreen tree of the laurel family. Cinnamon imparts a sweet aromatic flavour to numerous dishes from around the world, especially in European, Middle Eastern and Indian cuisine.

Cloves

The dried, nail-shaped buds from the neat evergreen tree with aromatic pink buds. These buds, when hand-picked and dried, turn reddish brown to become the cloves with which we are familiar. Good cloves should have a strong, pungent aroma and flavour and should be well-formed, plump and oily. Cloves have diverse uses in different cuisines of the world, being used for cakes, tarts and pastries, fancy rice dishes, soup stocks, sweet cooked fruits and in various spice blends.

Coconut Milk

Known as *santan* in Indonesian cooking, this creamy white liquid with a fresh coconut flavour is extracted from fresh coconut pulp and is used in a variety of South-East Asian and Indonesian dishes. It is available in cans from supermarkets and Asian grocers.

Concasse

A French culinary term literally meaning chopped or crushed, as in tomato *concasse*.

Conchiglie Gigante

An extra large conch-shaped pasta, especially suited to stuffing.

Coriander Leaves

The fresh leaves of the hardy annual plant *Coriandrum sativum*. Coriander is one of the most commonly used flavouring herbs in the world, certainly on par with parsley. It is known as *har dhania* in India and *cilantro* in Spanish-speaking countries. Bunches of coriander can be recognised by their smell and their fan-like lower leaves and feathery upper leaves.

Coriander Seeds

The round, brownish seeds of the annual herb *coriandrum sativum*, with a warm distinctive fragrance and a mild, sweet slightly pungent flavour reminiscent of a combination of sage and lemon. Available whole or ground, coriander adds a non-assertive flavour to many dishes from around the world, especially from India, Middle Eastern and Latin American cuisines.

Cornmeal

(see *polenta*)

Cumin Seeds

The oval, yellowish brown seeds of the plant *Cuminum cyminum* that are similar in appearance to caraway seeds. They have a warm, strongly aromatic and slightly bitter flavour, and are used extensively in Indian, Middle Eastern and Latin American cuisines, especially in Mexican dishes. The flavour and aroma of cumin, like most spice seeds, emerges best after they have been dry roasted or added to hot oil. In Indian cuisine, cumin is popular in yogurt-based salads, *dal* dishes and savouries.

Curd Cheese

The simplest type of unripened cheese, produced by adding an acidic curdling agent to boiled raw milk. This versatile, high protein food ingredient can also be used as a substitute for tofu, although it is sweeter and creamier. It can be pan-fried, deep-fried and added to juicy vegetable dishes, crumbled into salads, kneaded and rolled into small balls, and made into confectionery.

Curdle, to

When small amounts of acidic substances are added to hot milk, a protein known as casein coagulates and forms solid lumps known commonly as curd. Other proteins, principal among them lacto-globulin, remain suspended in the liquid, known as whey.

Curry Leaves

The thin, shiny, dark-green leaves of the South-East Asian tree *Murraya koenigii*. Curry leaves are highly aromatic when fresh. Used especially in South Indian kitchens, they are generally sautéed in oil with mustard seeds and asafetida and added to *dal*, fresh coconut chutney or vegetable dishes. Dried leaves are inferior, but are sometimes all that is available. Obtain curry leaves from Indian grocers.

Daikon Radish

A large white winter radish, also known as Japanese radish or *mooli*. It has a fresh, slightly peppery taste and a clean, crisp texture that makes it an ideal salad ingredient, although it can also be steamed or stir-fried. Daikon is available at well-stocked Asian food stores or vegetable markets.

Dal

A generic name for all members of the dried pea and bean family, and also the name of the thick, gravy-like or thin soup-like dishes made from them. *Dal*, besides being a good source of iron and B vitamins, is an excellent source of vegetable protein.

Dariole Mould

A small bucket-shaped mould used to make individual desserts.

Dill

A medium-sized herb with small feathery leaves and yellow flowers that's related to anise, caraway, coriander, cumin, fennel and parsley. Dill is an excellent partner for potatoes.

(to) Dry Roast

This technique refers to the process of slowly browning whole spice seeds, split *dal*, nuts and seeds and some types of flour. It is best done in a heavy pan or griddle that has been pre-warmed over low heat. The ingredients are stir-fried, without the addition of any oil or liquid, until lightly browned, releasing flavourful volatile oils and aromatic fragrances.

Emping

The kernel and horny covering around the fruit of the Indonesian *melinjo* tree. It is rolled flat and sundried for use as a fried snack or garnish, known as *krupuk emping* (*krupuk* means cracker).

Farfalle

Small pasta pieces made in the shape of a bow tie or butterfly.

Fennel Seeds

The oval, greenish or yellowish-brown

seeds of the hardy perennial of the parsley family have an agreeable, warm and sweet anise-like fragrance. Fennel seeds are one of the five spice seeds in the Bengali spice mix *panch porun*.

Feta

The white, dry crumbly cheese made from cow, ewe or goats' milk, cut into blocks and matured in brine to give it a sharp, acidic and salty taste. *Fete* is the Greek word for block or slice.

Filo

A pastry rolled out so thin that it is translucent, usually sold ready prepared in layers of several rectangular sheets. It originated in Turkey and travelled into central Europe during the spread of the Ottoman Empire. It is used in many Balkan and Middle Eastern specialties, both savoury and sweet.

Fried Bean Curd

There are a number of forms of deep-fried bean curd (tofu). Unless it is to be added to a broth or sauce, all deep-fried tofu needs to be reconstituted first. Japanese deep-fried tofu should be rinsed in boiling water before use. Pricking the tofu all over with a fork before adding to a broth helps it absorb flavour. Deep-fried tofu adds a rich 'meaty' taste to vegetarian soups and simmered dishes. Available at Asian grocers.

Gai Lan

Also known as Chinese broccoli, this popular member of the *Brassica* family has dark green leaves, stout stems and small white flowers. It often appears as a dish in its own right at banquets, where it is usually lightly boiled and served with a sauce.

Galangal

Aromatic roots in the same family as ginger. Of the two main varieties (greater and lesser *galangal*) greater *galangal* is more commonly used as a culinary adjunct. It resembles ginger in appearance, but its flavour is different, with an aroma reminiscent of camphor. The fresh root is much denser than ginger, and if at all mature it requires a sharp cleaver to cut it. *Galangal* is available as fresh roots, sliced and preserved in brine, as dried slices and in a powdered form.

Garam Masala

A blend of dry-roasted and ground spices well-used in Indian cuisine. The spices used in *garam masala* warm the body (*garam* means warm). Such spices include dried chilies, black pepper, cardamom, coriander, cinnamon, cloves and cumin. Many other spices are also added according to the region, since Indian cooking varies immensely according to the geographical location. Generally, *garam masala* is added towards the end of cooking. Various *garam masalas* can be purchased at Indian grocery stores.

Gari

Ginger slices that have been pickled in salt and sweet vinegar. They are a delicate pink colour and come in jars or plastic pouches at Asian grocers. Small amounts of *gari* are eaten between bites of *sushi* to freshen the palate.

Ghee

The oil produced by clarifying butter over gentle heat until all the moisture is driven off and the milk solids are fully separated from the clear butterfat. The essential difference between ghee and clarified butter, or butter oil, is that in the preparation of ghee, the solids (milk proteins and salts) are allowed to brown before being removed, thus imparting a nutty flavour. Ghee is an excellent choice for sautéeing and frying, and is much favoured in Indian cooking, as well as some French and Arabian Gulf cuisines. Ghee can be purchased at Indian or Middle Eastern grocery stores or well-stocked supermarkets.

Ginger

The thick, white tuberous underground stems or rhizomes of the plant *Zingiber officinale*, which thrives in the tropical areas of the world. Fresh ginger root has a spicy, sweet aroma and a hot clean taste, and is used in many cuisines, especially throughout China, Japan, Thailand and India. Young green ginger is especially appreciated for its fibre-free texture and mild flavour. Fresh ginger root is available at produce markets, Asian grocery stores and some supermarkets.

Glutinous Rice

Also known as sticky rice, glutinous rice can either be white or black, short or long grain. The Chinese and Japanese prefer the short grain variety, while in Thailand, long grain glutinous rice is preferred. White sticky rice is used primarily in sweet dishes throughout Asia, with the exception being the mountain areas of northern Thailand, Cambodia and Laos, where long grain sticky rice is the staple.

Grenadine

A sweet, tart red fruit syrup made from pomegranate juice. Available at Middle Eastern grocers.

Haloumi

A popular soft or semi-hard cheese with a salty, lactic flavour. *Haloumi* is made from the milk of sheep or goats and popular in Greece and the Middle East. It is heated in whey until boiling point, drained, then salted and preserved in salted whey. *Haloumi* is available at well-stocked specialty stores or Middle Eastern grocers.

Haricot Beans

These dried white beans are members of the *Phaseolus vulgaris* species and popular in stews, soups and casseroles.

They are well used in Italian cooking, and are available at grocery stores and supermarkets.

Hing
(see asafetida)

Hokkien Noodles
Plump, yellow wheat noodles that have been described as the spaghetti of the noodle world—thick and succulent, with a substantial 'meatiness' to them. Eggless varieties are easy to come by these days. They're perfect for quick, easy stir-fries, so it's good to have a packet in the fridge. They're generally sold vacuum-packed in plastic bags in the refrigerated section of Asian food stores or supermarkets.

Horseradish
A hardy perennial plant whose thick roots have a hot, pungent, white flesh that is grated as a cold garnish or to flavour other dishes. The outer root has a stronger flavour than the inner core, which is often discarded. Grated horseradish has a highly pungent penetrating odour plus volatile oils that cause tears to flow. Grated horseradish quickly loses its flavour, so it should be used immediately.

Jalapeño
One of the most well known chilies outside of Mexico. There are many varieties, but their shape is unmistakable—like an elongated, blunt triangle. *Jalapeños* are juicy, thick-fleshed with a clean, fresh, hot flavour, and range in colour from grass green to dark green or red. They are fairly hot and versatile.

Japanese Pepper
Known as *sansho*, it is one of the few spices used in Japanese cooking. Available at Japanese suppliers or well-stocked Asian grocers.

Jasmine Rice
(see Thai rice)

Jicama
(see yam bean)

(to) Julienne
To cut firm ingredients like vegetables, fruits, citrus rind, chilies or ginger root (to name but a few) into long, thin, matchstick strips or very fine shreds.

Kaffir Lime
The citrus fruit from the South-East Asian tree *Citrus hystrix* is not a true lime, but is picked in the immature state and is used as such. The rind is irregular and very bumpy with a pronounced smaller stem end. Although there is very little juice, the rind and leaves are a popular addition to curries, soups and salads. It is also known as *makrut* limes.

Kalamata Olives
Large, flavoursome and full-bodied ink-black to purple olives with pointed ends and shiny skins, named after the seaside town of southern Greece where they are grown. They are especially popular in Greek cuisine, but are used wherever olives are called for.

Kalonji
Also known as *nigella* or black onion seeds (no relation to the onion). Very often these jet-black, teardrop seeds are confused with, or called, black cumin seeds, which are a completely different spice altogether. *Kalonji* seeds have a peppery taste and a pleasant herbal aroma. They are sprinkled on Turkish pide breads, *naan* breads, and are an important ingredient in the Bengali five-spice blend *panch puran*. The seeds are available at Indian or Middle Eastern grocers.

Kangkong
Also known as water spinach, swamp cabbage and water *convolvulus*, this leafy vegetable is prolific in many parts of Asia. The leaves are long, pointed and dark green, the stems paler green and hollow. It is cooked like spinach, stir-fried with various sauces, added to soups or washed thoroughly and used raw in salads. Available at Asian greengrocers.

Kecap Manis
A thick sweet soy sauce from Indonesia.

Kidney Beans
These popular kidney-shaped beans from the plant *Phaseolus vulgaris* are used extensively. They make a good substitute for *borlotti* beans in Italian cooking, as an alternative to pinto beans in Mexican cuisine, or in soups stews and casseroles. Kidney beans are also a popular ingredient in the Punjab where they are known as *rajma*.

Kombu
Dried kelp. This sea vegetable is available in the form of hard, flat, black sheets that have a fine white powder on their surface. *Kombu* is used to flavour *dashi*, a basic Japanese soup stock, and *sushi* rice. Wipe the surface of the *kombu* sheets before use to remove the powder. Do not wash the *kombu* as this will diminish the flavour. Avoid *kombu* that is wrinkled and thin.

Krupuk
(see *emping*)

Laksa Leaf
(see Vietnamese mint)

Lemongrass
A tall lemon-scented grass with narrow, sharp-edged leaves and a central rib. Lemongrass imparts a pleasant lemon fragrance to soups and curries, and is one of the most popular herbs of South-East Asia.
The bulbous lower stem, creamy-white to pale green, is the part used, and can be sliced cross-wise or bruised with a mallet and simmered whole in a dish. The leaves also make a refreshing tea.

Lentils

Used extensively in many cuisines of the world. Brown lentils from the plant *Lens culinaris*, and red lentils (called *masoor dal* in India) are probably the most well known.

Lime Leaves

(see *kaffir* lime)

Mangosteen

A small, slow-growing tree native to Malaysia which bears round fruit with a thick, dark purple shell. The fruit is divided into small white segments that are thirst quenching and sweet with a hint of sourness.

Maple Syrup

A sweet syrup prepared from the sap of the sugar maple tree *Acer saccharum* which is collected by boring a hole into the trunk. Used extensively as a sweetener, especially in North America.

(to) Marinate

A procedure during which foods are soaked in a liquid mixture, called a marinade, to either preserve the food, infuse them with flavour or tenderise them.

Masala

A combination of herbs, spices or seasonings used in Indian cuisine. Some *masalas*, like Bengali *panch puran*, contain whole spices. Others like *chat masala* and *garam masala*, *sambar masala* or *rasam* powder, contain numerous powdered spices combined together.

Mesclun

A combination of tiny salad leaves.

Mint

A widely-used culinary herb. There are many varieties, but mint may be generally described as having a fresh, strong, sweet and tangy flavour with a cool after-taste.

Millet

There are many members of the millet family, although common millet is the one used in this book. Millet is a tiny, buff-coloured nutritious grain about the size of a mustard seed with a delicate, bland flavour. It is generally toasted before cooking, and takes on nutty flavour overtones in the process.

Mozzarella Cheese

This famous spun-curd Italian cheese was traditionally made from buffalo's milk, but these days it is frequently made from cow's milk. It is formed in a round or pear shape, and becomes characteristically stringy when cooked.

Mung Badis

(see *badis*)

Mung Beans

Slightly oval, small beans with olive-green skins. They are quick to cook, and don't require soaking beforehand. They are easy to digest and rich in iron and protein. Mung beans are commonly used in Indian soups and stews, as well as in Vietnamese and Thai cuisine. The whole beans are available at well-stocked supermarkets. Split and skinless yellow mung beans are available at Asian suppliers.

Mung Bean Shoots

Sprouted whole green mung beans. In Chinese cooking, the mung beans are allowed to sprout until quite long. However, from a nutritional point of view, mung sprouts are best used when just shooted and the sprout is less than 1cm long. Sprouted mung beans are rich in vitamins B, C and E, and are 37 per cent protein (their protein content is highly digestible). They are pleasantly sweet, low in calories and inexpensive.

Mustard Seeds

Of the many varieties of mustard, three of them are most prominent: the tiny round blackish-brown seeds from the plant known as *Brassica nigra* (commonly known as black mustard), the purple-brown seeds of *Brassica juncea* (commonly called brown mustard) and the yellow seeds from *Brassica alba* (known as white or yellow mustard). The two darker varieties are commonly used as a seasoning in India. The yellow variety are less pungent and are commonly used in European cuisine.

New Mexico Chilies

A full-bodied, mildly-hot chili from Mexico and the southern US (sometimes referred to as Colorado or California Chili).

Nori

Sheets of seaweed used for making *sushi*. The sheets measure about 19 x 20 cm (7½ x 8 inches) and are sold in cellophane or plastic bags in all Asian grocers. Once the packet has been opened, use the *nori* as soon as possible or store it in a container in a cool place. Make sure you purchase precooked *nori*, known as *yaki-nori*, which is dark green. The black or purple types of *nori* are raw and must be toasted over a flame.

Nutmeg

The fragrant nut found in the centre of the densely foliated evergreen tree *Myristica fragrans*. The fleshy fruit of the nutmeg tree resembles an apricot. When it is ripe, it splits in half, revealing the beautiful, brilliant scarlet, net-like membrane known as mace. It closely enwraps the brittle shell containing the glossy-brown oily nutmeg. Nutmeg imparts a warm, sweet and highly spicy flavour to a variety of dishes around the world.

Oatmeal

The hulled oat grain that has been rolled or cut into flakes.

Okra

The seed pod of the plant *Abelmoschus*

esculentus, used when young as a vegetable, or when mature, dried and powdered as a flavouring. Okra, also known as *bindi* or ladyfinger, is grown in most hot areas of the world.

Olive oil

The oil extracted from the fruits of the Mediterranean tree *Olea europea*. The finest olive oil is cold-pressed from fresh, ripe olives and has a pale yellow or greenish colour. Cruder versions of olive oil are second pressings made under heat. Choosing olive oil is a matter of personal taste and preference.

Oregano

A piquant herb famous in Greek and Italian cuisine. It is excellent with any tomato dish, especially pizza, and varieties of pasta dishes. Its flavour marries well with basil.

Palm Sugar

A dark brown sugar produced by boiling down the sap of various palm trees. Palm sugar has a rich, sweet taste and is an appropriate sweetener in various South-East Asian and Indonesian dishes. It is sold in thick, tubular sections or round lumps, and is available from Asian grocers.

Pandan Leaves

Also known as *pandanus* leaves. These long, thin green leaves are popular in Malaysia, Sri Lanka, Indonesia and Thailand as an important flavouring agent for both savoury and sweet dishes. The flavour of *pandan* is aromatic and delicate and is as important to Asians as vanilla is to Westerners. Fresh *pandan* leaves are available at Asian grocers frozen, and sometimes fresh.

(to) Pan-fry

The technique of frying any ingredient in a small amount of oil.

Panir

(see curd cheese)

Pappadams

Sundried, paper-thin wafers made from wet-ground mung or *urad* beans. In India they are most popular flame-toasted until crispy and eaten before or after dinner. They can also be deep-fried.
Paprika
The bright red powder made from the dried, sweet chili pepper pods of the many varieties of *Capsicum anuum*. Good paprika has a brilliant red colour, and because it is not hot, it is often used in generous quantities, giving dishes a rich red hue. It is also very nutritious, having a high vitamin C content.

Parmesan

The most famous of all the *grana* or matured, hard cheeses of Italy. Parmesan *(parmigiano)* takes at least two years to come to maturity, resulting in its traditional sharp flavour. Parmesan cheese should be bought in pieces to be freshly grated over sauces, pasta or rice, or added to cooked dishes.

Parsley

Parsley is one of the best known and most extensively used culinary herbs in Western cuisine. There are numerous cultivated varieties of parsley, but the ornamental curled variety is the most popular as a garnish, and the flat-leaved parsley, known also as continental parsley, is the most favoured in Italian and other Mediterranean cuisines. Parsley is a pleasant addition to an enormous variety of savoury dishes.

Penne

Short tubes of pasta cut about 4cm (2-inches) long on the diagonal to resemble quill pens.

Pepper

The small, round berries from the woody, perennial evergreen vine, *Piper nigrum*. Black pepper, white pepper and green pepper are all obtained from these same berries at different stages of their maturity. Black and white pepper are used in practically every cuisine of the world. Although available pre-ground, freshly-ground pepper from a mill has the best flavour.

Pesto

Referred to as *pistou* in France, this famous pungent sauce is made primarily of fresh basil leaves, Parmesan cheese and toasted pine nuts. Many variations on this theme using different nuts and herbs are now becoming popular.

Pide

A thick Turkish flat bread.

Pine nuts

Also known as pine kernels, *pignolia*, or *pinoli*. Pine nuts come from the cone of the stone pine, a tree native to the Mediterranean. Their buttery flavour is intensified when they are lightly toasted.

Pinto Beans

A variety of pale kidney bean *Phaseolus vulgaris* with bright red markings, popular in Spain, Mexico and North America.

Pita

Popular yeasted round flat breads that can be opened into pockets.

Polenta

Polenta is a yellow maize or cornmeal grown in Northern Italy, where it is regarded as a staple food. It is graded according to its texture and available in fine, medium or coarse-ground. You can purchase *polenta* at most supermarkets and health food stores.

Pomegranate Molasses

A thick, dark and sour syrup produced from boiling down pomegranate juice. Used for flavouring various Middle Eastern dishes. Available at Middle Eastern grocers, it is not to be confused with pomegranate syrup (*grenadine*) which is sweet.

Pomegranate Syrup
(see grenadine)

Prasadam
Food that has been offered to God before being eaten. *Prasadam* means 'God's mercy'.

Pulao
The terms *pulao*, *pilau* and *pilaff* refer to classical rice dishes where dry rice is fried in oil or butter until it becomes translucent before liquid is added. The oil impregnates the outer layers of the grains and helps keep them separate while cooking.

Ramekin
A small, individual circular porcelain, earthenware or glass oven-proof dish.

Rennet
Rennet is an enzyme used in cheese making which coagulates milk proteins, thus setting the curd. The first step in cheese making is the addition of a starter culture of *Streptococci* and *Lactobacilli*. These bacteria ferment the lactose to lactic acid and reduce the milk's pH to the proper range for the rennet to coagulate the proteins. The rennet is added at this stage. The active enzyme in rennet, called *rennin*, is remarkably efficient. In pure form, one part will coagulate 5 million parts of milk.

The problem for strict vegetarians is that most cheese manufacturers use a rennet derived from the fourth or true stomach of a milk-fed calf. The good news is that although calves' stomachs are the classic source of rennet, there are alternatives. Many cheeses produced in Australia now come with 'non-animal rennet' listed with the ingredients. That means the manufacturers have used herbal, microbial or synthetic rennet to make their cheese.

Rice Vermicelli
Probably the world's most versatile noodle, rice vermicelli, also known as rice sticks, are thin, dried, brittle white noodles made from extruded rice flour paste. They give texture and contrast to a dish without adding too much bulk. Known in Cantonese as *mai fun*, in Mandarin as *mi fen*, in Thailand as *sen mee*, and in Malaysia as *behoon*.

Ricotta Cheese
A soft crumbly white cheese made from the whey of cow's milk and popular in Italian cuisine. It is frequently used in cooking both sweet and savoury dishes in Italy, for like curd cheese or cottage cheese its mild, somewhat bland flavour combines well with other ingredients. It is available at selected supermarkets or grocers.

Risotto
The rice eaten throughout Northern Italy. Authentic *risotto* should be prepared only with a variety of Italian *superfino* rice such as *arborio*. In *risotto* cooking, the rice is first coated in butter, then cooked slowly with the gradual addition of stock, and stirred continuously until the stock is absorbed and the rice is soft, with a gentle coating of sauce.

Rocket
Also known as *arugula*, *roquette*, *ruccola* and *rughetta*. A small, green, leafy plant resembling radish tops that grow wild in the Mediterranean region. Rocket leaves have a peppery, slightly bitter, slightly acidic flavour.

Rosemary
The small, narrow aromatic leaves of the evergreen shrub *Rosmarinus officinalis*. This fragrant seasoning herb has a clean, woody odour reminiscent of pine.

Rosewater
The diluted essence of rose petals, particularly from the highly scented species *Rosa damascena* and *Rosa centifolia*. It is widely used throughout the Middle East and India as a flavouring agent. It is available at Middle Eastern and Indian grocers.

Salsa
The word literally means sauce in Spanish. Outside of Spanish speaking countries, *salsa* refers to a sauce or relish made with freshly chopped uncooked ingredients, usually tomatoes, with the addition of herb, fresh chilies and sometimes a little lime or lemon juice.

Saffron
The slender dried stigmas of the flowers of *Crocus sativus*. About 210,000 hand-picked stigmas are needed to make half a kilogram (1 pound) saffron, making it the world's most expensive spice. The dried threads are dark orange to reddish-brown with a pleasantly spicy, pungent, slightly bitter, honey-like taste. Saffron is used today in Indian, French, Middle Eastern and Spanish cooking.

Sambal Oelek
A hot condiment made from ground, fresh hot red chilies, and popular in Malay and Indonesian cuisine. It is often added to a dish for an extra hot chili dimension or served as an accompaniment. Available at Asian grocery stores.

Sansho
(see Japanese pepper)

Semolina
The cream-coloured cereal obtained from hard durum wheat grains in the middle stages of flour milling, when the wheat germ, bran, and endosperm are separated. Semolina, also known as *farina*, is popular worldwide.

Sesame Seeds

The cream to black seeds from the seed pods of the annual plant *Sesamum indicum*, grown pre-dominantly in India and China. The flat, pear-shaped seeds are generally lightly roasted to bring out their nutty flavour and are a popular ingredient worldwide.

Snake Beans

Known by various names, including asparagus bean, Chinese long bean and yard bean. These narrow, round-bodied beans are dark-green, stringless and approximately 30–40cm (12–16 inches) long. They taste similar to green beans, but have a denser texture. They are available at Indian and Asian vegetable markets.

Sorrel

The word 'sorrel' is derived from the old teutonic word for sour. Sorrel, which shares the same family as rhubarb, has a refreshing, somewhat bitter, sour, spinach-like flavour. It should always be cooked for a minimum time to preserve its fresh flavour. If used raw in salads, select only young, tender leaves.

Sticky Rice

(see glutinous rice)

Sticky Rice Flour

A fine white flour made from glutinous rice and used to make soft cakes, buns and dumplings in Asian and South-East Asian cooking.

Srila Prabhupada

The Founder-Acharya (spiritual master) of the International Society for Krishna Consciousness (ISKCON). His Divine Grace A. C. Bhaktivedanta Swami Prabhupada was the author of many spiritual texts, and the world's most distinguished teacher of Vedic religion and thought.

Sushi Vinegar

A mild-tasting vinegar made from rice that is specifically made for *sushi*. Other vinegars cannot be substituted as they are too strong.

Sumac

An important souring agent in Arab cuisine. The seeds of *Rhus corioria* are ground to a purple-red powder and used to add a sour, pleasantly astringent taste to recipes as a preferred substitute for lemon. *Sumac*'s pleasant, rounded, fruity sourness which is well worth experimenting with.

Tahini

A semi-liquid sesame butter used in Middle Eastern cuisine. This cream-grey paste has the consistency of runny peanut butter and is the basis of various salad dressings and *mezze* (entrées) throughout Greece, Cyprus, Lebanon, Jordan and Syria.

Tamarind

The pulp extracted from the brown pods of the tamarind tree, *Tamarindus indica*. The fresh pulp has a sour, fruity taste and is popular in South-East Asian and Indian cooking. Tamarind comes in the form of blocks of partly dried, unpitted pods, slightly more refined paste, concentrate, and liquid purée. Choose whichever is most appropriate for the recipe that includes it.

Tempe

Yellow-brown cakes of compressed, culture-innoculated fermented whole soya beans. A white soft coating, similar to that which covers cheese like *brie* or *camambert*, forms over the cakes, holding the grains together. The texture of *tempe* is soft-cruchy, and nutritionally, *tempe* is high in easily assimilated proteins and low in cholesterol. *Tempe* is particularly popular in Indonesian cuisine.

Thai Rice

A long grain aromatic white rice from Thailand that is also referred to as jasmine rice. It cooks to large, soft fluffy grains.

Thyme

An attractive herb that imparts a distinctively warm aromatic flavour and is popular as one of the great European culinary herbs. It is used alongside bay and parsley in *bouquet garni*, and combines especially well with potatoes, zucchini, eggplants and capsicum (peppers).

Tofu

Soy bean curd or tofu is used in Chinese, Japanese, Korean and Indonesian cooking. This white, almost tasteless and odourless substance is produced from soya beans that have been successively crushed, boiled in water, strained and pressed into a mould. Tofu is low in calories and is cholesterol free. High in protein, tofu is becoming a common and extremely versatile ingredient in Western kitchens.

Tomatillos

The plant *Phyalis ixocarpa* yields golf-ball sized green fruits that turn yellow. The fruits are enclosed in a papery husk. *Tomatillos* are an essential ingredient in *salsa verde* and other Mexican recipes. If unavailable, substitute with green tomatoes.

Tortilla

Thin round flat breads made from white cornmeal, or *masa*. *Tortillas* are the national bread of Mexico and are cooked on a griddle. They're eaten fresh and are also the basis of other Mexican dishes such as *tostadas*, *enchiladas*, etc.

Turmeric

The rhizome, or underground stem, of the tropical herb *Curcuma longa*. The short, waxy, orange-yellow rhizomes are boiled, cleaned, sundried and then ground to a fine aromatic, yellow powder that is used as an essential ingredient in Asian and Indian cooking. Turmeric adds a brilliant yellow colour to cooked dishes and imparts a slightly bitter, musty-pungent flavour.

Urad Dal

The split dried beans from the plant *Phaseolus mungo*. They are used to prepare protein-rich purées, dumplings, pancakes and soups in Indian cooking. In South India they are also used as a seasoning and fried in oil with curry leaves, asafetida and mustard seeds.

Vanilla

The pod of the climbing tropical orchid, *Vanilla plantifolia*. The vanilla flavouring material is obtained from the dried, cured, partially ripe pods. The white crystalline compound called vanillin, present only in the cured pods, provides the delicately sweet, rich and spicy aroma which characterises vanilla.

Vietnamese Mint

This pungently flavoured herb is not a true mint, but is widely known by this common name. It is also known as Cambodian mint, hot mint, *laksa* leaf, *daun laksa* and *daun kesom*. It has a distinctive peppery flavour and is popular in Vietnamese cooking where it is eaten raw as a salad accompaniment.

Water Chestnuts

Fresh water chestnuts, with their crunchy succulent texture and sweet, nutty taste are a common delicacy in Asian cuisine. They are actually the edible root of an aquatic plant. Fresh water chestnuts are sometimes available at Asian grocers. The canned variety is an acceptable substitute.

Water Convulvulus

(see *kangkong*)

Wheat Vermicelli

A pasta resembling very fine spaghetti.

Whey

The liquid by-product when milk is curdled in the curd-cheese making process, or from yogurt when it is allowed to drain in a cheesecloth.

Wonton Wrapper

Squares or rounds of noodle dough dusted in cornflour and available fresh or frozen in Asian grocers.

Yam Beans

Known also as sweet turnip, as well as its Mexican name *jicama* (pronounced 'hee-kama'). These disc-shaped tubers have a pleasantly crunchy white flesh which is slightly sweet and juicy and can be both cooked like a water chestnut or eaten fresh as a fruit.

Zest

The outer skin of an orange or lemon that is pared thinly to give flavour to various dishes.

Index

About the Author

Kurma Dasa was born in England, moving to Australia with his parents in 1964. He started his cooking career in the Sydney kitchens of the Hare Krishna movement, where he began by cutting vegetables, grinding fresh herbs and spices, and assisting in the preparation of their famous Sunday Feasts.

Since those humble beginnings, Kurma has gone on to teach his special brand of elegant and eclectic gourmet vegetarian cuisine throughout Australia and around the world.

Kurma was head chef at Melbourne's most popular Vegetarian Restaurant, *Gopal's* for many years, and is the author of *Great Vegetarian Dishes* which is in its seventh print run, *Cooking With Kurma*, and most recently *Quick Vegetarian Dishes*. Kurma's books have received wide acclaim for their professional, clearly written and richly illustrated presentation of vegetarian cuisine.

Kurma has hosted three internationally broadcast television cooking series seen in over 46 countries. His third and latest 26-part TV series *More Great Vegetarian Dishes* currently screens throughout Australia on SBS and Foxtel.

Kurma's light-hearted presentation of healthy, delicious, attractive and innovative cuisine continues to shake off the outdated notion that vegetarian food is dull and lacklustre. Currently, Kurma is presenting gourmet vegetarian cooking masterclasses Australia-wide, writing columns for various magazines and working on more cookbooks. Kurma lives in Perth with his wife, Ananda, and young son Nitai.

If you wish to correspond with the author, please write to him at:

PO Box 102 Bayswater, Western Australia 6053, Australia
(e-mail: kurma@com.org)

Other Books by the Author

Great Vegetarian Dishes

Over 240 receipes from around the world, each tested and refined by Kurma Dasa. This 192 page beautifully presented cookbook features over 100 stunning full-colour photos.

A$27.45 (incl GST, postage & packing)

Cooking with Kurma

Kurma Dasa's second best selling cookbook presents *More Great Vegetarian Dishes*. 256 pages in full glorious colour.

A$38.45 (incl GST, postage & packing)

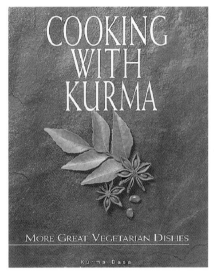

Special offer

Order both Titles for the Special Package Price of A$55.00 (incl GST, postage and packing)

offer only valid in Australia

---------------Cut ✂--

YES please send me the following:

Great Vegetarian Dishes___ Cooking with Kurma___ Both Titles___

for a total of $ _____

Payment may be made by Cheque or Credit Card

Card Number _____

Expiry Date: _____

Signature of Card Holder _____

Send along with payment to Bhaktivedant Book Trust, P.O. Box 262, Botany, NSW 1455

Name_____

Address_____

City _____ State _____

Pincode _____

Home Phone _____